Teaching with Reverence

Teaching with Reverence

Reviving an Ancient Virtue for Today's Schools

Edited by

A. G. Rud and Jim Garrison

TEACHING WITH REVERENCE
Copyright © A. G. Rud and Jim Garrison, 2012.

All rights reserved.

Billy Collins, excerpt from "Schoolsville" from *The Apple That Astonished Paris*. Copyright © 1988, 1996 by Billy Collins. Reprinted with the permission of The Permissions Company, Inc. on behalf of the University of Arkansas Press, www.uapress.com.

First published in 2012 by
PALGRAVE MACMILLAN®
in the United States—a division of St. Martin's Press LLC,
175 Fifth Avenue, New York, NY 10010.

Where this book is distributed in the UK, Europe and the rest of the world, this is by Palgrave Macmillan, a division of Macmillan Publishers Limited, registered in England, company number 785998, of Houndmills, Basingstoke, Hampshire RG21 6XS.

Palgrave Macmillan is the global academic imprint of the above companies and has companies and representatives throughout the world.

Palgrave® and Macmillan® are registered trademarks in the United States, the United Kingdom, Europe and other countries.

ISBN: 978–0–230–11492–0

Library of Congress Cataloging-in-Publication Data

　　Teaching with reverence : reviving an ancient virtue for today's schools / [edited by] A.G. Rud and Jim Garrison.
　　　p. cm.
　　　ISBN 978–0–230–11492–0
　　　1. Moral education—United States. 2. Values—Study and teaching—United States. I. Rud, A. G., 1953– II. Garrison, James W., 1949– III.Title.

LC311.T435 2012
370.11′40973—dc23   2011031582

A catalogue record of the book is available from the British Library.

Design by Newgen Imaging Systems (P) Ltd., Chennai, India.

First edition: January 2012

10 9 8 7 6 5 4 3 2 1

Transferred to Digital Printing in 2013

To the late Rachael Kessler, who was to have joined us in reflecting on reverence in teaching. Her book The Soul of Education *and the ongoing work of the PassageWorks Institute she founded continue to inspire reverence for teaching in the lives of many people.*

Contents

Acknowledgments   ix

List of Contributors   xi

Introduction: Teaching with Reverence: Reviving an Ancient Virtue for Today's Schools   1
A. G. Rud and Jim Garrison

1   The Practice of Reverent Teaching   17
Robert Boostrom

2   Reverence and Love in Teaching   33
Daniel P. Liston

3   "To Seek by Way of Silence"   49
Michael Dale

4   "Spots of Time That Glow": Reverence, Epiphany, and the Teaching Life   61
Sam M. Intrator

5   Awakening Reverence: The Role of Descriptive Inquiry in Developing Perception and Reverence—The Case of the Prospect School Teacher Education Program   79
Carol Rodgers

6   Risking Reverence   97
Elaine J. O'Quinn

7   Reverence for What? A Teacher's Quest   113
William H. Schubert

8   Lesson One: Reverence   129
William Ayers

9 Quotidian Sublimity 137
   Megan J. Laverty

10 Reverence for Things Not Seen: Implied Creators in
   Works of Art, Implied Teachers in Creative Pedagogy 153
   Bruce Novak

Index 167

Acknowledgments

This book is part of a larger research and writing project on reverence and education based initially on our enthusiasm for Paul Woodruff's book, *Reverence: Renewing a Forgotten Virtue*. We collaborated on conference presentations and a number of articles, some of which are listed in the references to the introduction. Many people have shared their thoughts with us along the way. We are part of a research group on the importance of listening in education, led by Sophie Haroutunian-Gordon of Northwestern University, where we presented some of our early ideas for this book. We thank that hospitable group that remains productive to this day. The authors thank Rita Rud for her expert editing and advice on the manuscript, and the editorial team at Palgrave Macmillan of Samantha Hasey and Kaylan Connally. Our editor at Palgrave Macmillan, Burke Gerstenschlager, believed in the project from the beginning and understood what we were trying to do. Finally, we thank all of our authors for working so well with us, for their fine contributions, and for helping us think more creatively and reflectively about the important and neglected topic of reverence in teaching.

Contributors

William Ayers recently retired as distinguished professor of education and senior university scholar at the University of Illinois at Chicago, and founder of both the Small Schools Workshop and the Center for Youth and Society, where he taught courses in interpretive and qualitative research, urban school change, and teaching and the modern predicament. Ayers has written extensively about social justice, democracy, and education, the cultural contexts of schooling, and teaching as an essentially intellectual, ethical, and political enterprise. His books include *Teaching Toward Freedom: Moral Commitment and Ethical Action in the Classroom* (Beacon Press, 2004), *Teaching the Personal and the Political: Essays on Hope and Justice* (Teachers College Press, 2004), and *To Teach: The Journey of a Teacher* (Teachers College Press, 1993), which was named Book of the Year in 1993 by Kappa Delta Pi, and won the Witten Award for Distinguished Work in Biography and Autobiography in 1995.

Robert Boostrom is professor of teacher education and licensing advisor at the University of Southern Indiana, where he has taught since 1993. Coauthor (with Philip Jackson and David Hansen) of *The Moral Life of Schools* (Jossey-Bass, 1993), he is also author of *Thinking: The Foundation of Creative and Critical Learning in the Classroom* (Teachers College Press, 2005). He has been an Associate Editor of the *Journal of Curriculum Studies* since 1997. Most recently, he has been interested in play (in all of its forms, from children's rough-and-tumble play to adults' complex games, from humor to music, from athletic contests to religious practices) as a neglected dimension of thinking and schooling. This is a topic he took up, as president of the American Association for Teaching and Curriculum, in the 2009 Presidential Address, "Why I am not wearing a tie: Some thoughts about experience and judgment" (which appears in the 2010 issue of *Curriculum and Teaching Dialogue*).

Michael Dale is a professor of philosophy of education and a teacher educator at Appalachian State University in Boone, NC. He received his Ph.D.

in philosophy of education from the University of Wisconsin-Madison. His interests include the relationships between philosophy and literature, literature and emotions, and how engagement with novels and short stories provides an opening for exploring and examining meaningful issues and questions about learning, teaching, and human relationships. Most recently, he published with Elizabeth M. Frye "Vulnerability and Love of Learning as Necessities for Wise Teacher Education" in the *Journal of Teacher Education*. In addition to teaching undergraduate and graduate courses in the college of education, he maintains a longtime commitment to conducting a one-year seminar course in the Heltzer Honors Program at Appalachian State University where he has been teaching for twenty-three years.

Jim Garrison is a professor of philosophy of education at Virginia Tech in Blacksburg, Virginia, holding appointments, in addition, in the department of philosophy, the science, technology, and society program, and the alliance for social, political, ethical, and cultural thought. His work concentrates on philosophical pragmatism. He is a former president of the Philosophy of Education Society as well as the John Dewey Society, and president-elect of the Society of Professors of Education (founded in 1902). Jim has recently completed a series of twenty dialogues with Daisaku Ikeda, president of Soka Gakkai International, and Larry Hickman, head of the Center for Dewey Studies, that appear monthly in *Todi* magazine. He is the author or editor of nine books, including the most recently edited works: *Reconstructing Democracy, Recontextualizing Dewey* (SUNY Press, 2008), and *John Dewey at One Hundred-Fifty: Reflections for a New Century* with A. G. Rud and Lynda Stone (Purdue University Press, 2009).

Sam M. Intrator came to Smith College in 1999 after more than a decade of teaching and administrative service in public schools in Brooklyn, Vermont, and California. He has a Ph.D. from Stanford University and a master's degree in from the Bread Loaf School of English. Intrator teaches courses on urban education, youth development, and the teaching of humanities in K-12 schools. Intrator has written or edited five books that have sold over 125,000 copies including *Tuned in and Fired Up: How Teaching Can Inspire Real Learning in the Classroom* (Yale University Press, 2003), which was a finalist for the prestigious $200,000 Grawemeyer Award in Education. His latest book *Leading from Within: Poetry that Sustains the Courage to Lead* (Jossey-Bass, 2007) received several awards including a 2007 Best Business Book award by 800-CEO-READ and a 2009 Nautilus Book Award for Poetry. He has received a number of awards including a Presidential Distinguished Teacher Award by the White Commission on Presidential Scholars, a Kellogg National Leadership Fellowship, and an Ella Baker Fellowship.

Megan J. Laverty is associate professor in the Philosophy and Education Program at Teachers College, Columbia University. She has held appointments at Melbourne University in Australia and Montclair State University in the United States of America. She has held visiting appointments at the Australian Catholic University in Australia, Gyeongsang National University in South Korea and the Hong Kong Institute of Education in Hong Kong. She has published widely in such journals as *Educational Theory*, *Journal of Philosophy of Education*, *Theory and Research in Education*, *Journal of Ethics Education Studies*, and *Learning Inquiry*. She is the author of *Iris Murdoch's Ethics: A Consideration of her Romantic Vision* (Continuum, 2007) and coeditor of *Philosophy of Education: Modern and Contemporary Ideas at Play* (Kendall/Hunt, 2009). She researches within the area of moral philosophy, and her current focus is on language, communication, civility, and dialogue.

Daniel P. Liston is a professor of education and associate dean of graduate studies in the School of Education at the University of Colorado at Boulder. His past work includes numerous articles and several books on teacher education as well as the social and political context of schooling. Recently he served as the editor (with Jim Garrison) of *Teaching, Learning, and Loving* (RoutledgeFalmer, 2004) and as editor (with Hilda Borko and Jennie Whitcomb) of the *Journal of Teacher Education*. His current scholarship focuses on the role of reason and emotion in teaching, and the features of contemplative teaching. He is currently the Co-Director (with Paul Michalec) of Colorado Courage to Teach and Lead, a program of professional renewal for teachers, school and community leaders, and clergy.

Elaine J. O'Quinn is a professor of English education at Appalachian State University in Boone, NC. She is also a faculty member of Women's Studies where she recently developed a Girls' Studies minor. Her most recent work includes an edited book entitled *Girls' Literacy Experiences In and Out of School: Learning and Composing Gendered Identities* (Routledge, 2012). She has also published numerous articles and book chapters on teaching, adolescent literature, and girls studies. Her most recent publications include "Teacher, Writer, Revolutionary: A Parallel Journey" (in *Getting it in Writing: The Quest to Become an Outstanding and Effective Teacher of Writing*; Information Age, 2011) and "Picturing a Life: Lessons and Landscapes of an Iranian Girlhood" (*The Signal Journal*, February, 2011).

Bruce Novak is the author of *Literacy for Love and Wisdom: "Being the Book" and "Being the Change"* (with Jeffrey D. Wilhelm, Teachers College Press, 2011), a call for the reconstrual of "English" as "Personal Studies," a discipline of democratic humanism centered less on "the letter" than on "the human spirit." He has taught middle and high school English, helped prepare English teachers, and taught philosophy of education at the University of Chicago and Northern Illinois University. Currently he is the director of Educational Projects for the Foundation for Ethics and Meaning and an assistant professor of English education at Indiana University of Pennsylvania.

Carol Rodgers is an associate professor of education at the University at Albany, State University of New York. Her interests include reflective practice, John Dewey, presence in teaching, the inner life of the teacher, and the history of progressive teacher education. Her publications include "Defining reflection: Another look at John Dewey and reflective thinking," *Teachers College Record* (2002), which was given the AERA Award for Exemplary Research in 2004; "Seeing student learning: Teacher change and the role of reflection," *Harvard Educational Review* (2002); "Presence in teaching," *Teachers and Teaching: Theory and Practice* (2006, coauthored with Miriam Raider-Roth); "Attending to student voice," *Curriculum Inquiry* (2006); " 'The turning of one's soul': Lessons in race and social justice: The Putney Graduate School of Teacher Education," 1950-1965, *Teachers College Record* (2006), and Development of the personal self and professional identity in learning to teach. (Rodgers, C. and K. Scott. 2008. In *Handbook of Research in Teacher Education*. Edited by Marilyn Cochran-Smith and Sharon Feiman-Nemser. Mahwah, NJ: Lawrence Erlbaum).

A. G. Rud is dean and professor in the College of Education at Washington State University. He holds an A.B. in religion from Dartmouth College and M.A. and Ph.D. in philosophy from Northwestern University. Rud researches the moral dimensions of teaching, learning, and leading in both K-12 and higher education. His most recent book is *Albert Schweitzer's Legacy for Education: Reverence for Life*, published by Palgrave Macmillan in 2011. Rud has served as chair of the editorial board of Purdue University Press as well as a member of the editorial or review boards of notable educational journals such as *Educational Theory, Education Policy Analysis Archives, Journal of Thought,* and *Studies in Philosophy and Education.* He recently completed a six-year term as editor of *Education and Culture*, the journal of the John Dewey Society.

William H. Schubert is professor of education and university scholar at the University of Illinois at Chicago, where he coordinates the Ph.D.

Program in curriculum studies and has been recognized with several awards for teaching, mentoring, and scholarship. A former elementary teacher and frequent lecturer, he has published 16 books and over 150 articles and chapters. Schubert is former president of the John Dewey Society, the Society of Professors of Education, and the Society for the Study of Curriculum History; he is an elected member of the International Academy of Education and Professors of Curriculum, is associate editor of *Educational Theory*, and recipient of the 2004 American Educational Research Association Lifetime Achievement Award in Curriculum Studies, as well as the 2007 Mary Anne Raywid Award of the Society of Professors of Education. His most recent book is *Love, Justice, and Education: John Dewey and the Utopians* (Information Age, 2009).

Introduction: Teaching with Reverence: Reviving an Ancient Virtue for Today's Schools

A. G. Rud and Jim Garrison

Reverence is a largely forgotten virtue in American society. When we do remember it, we usually confine it narrowly to the religious domain and assume that the separation of church and state necessitates that we ignore it, at least in public schools. In a broader spiritual sense, it is often associated with a mute and prim solemnity. Even then, many think that spirituality has no place in schools. Reverence is also a forgotten virtue in teaching and learning (Rud and Garrison, 2010). Most can conceive of teaching only as about imparting skills and knowledge that will serve students well in career and life. However, the contributors to the present volume understand that there is much more to teaching students than merely imparting knowledge. They realize that good teaching involves forming character, molding destinies, creating an enduring passion for learning, appreciating beauty, respecting silence, caring for others, and much more. In some sense, teaching is a spiritual, although not necessarily a religious, activity. When done well, it paves the way for human sociability and intimacy and allows teachers to find creative self-expression in the classroom community. The chapters collected in this volume examine reverence as a way to understand some of the spiritual dimensions of classroom teaching.

Listen to the public rhetoric about schools and it becomes clear that the public ignores many things teachers find personally meaningful. When you listen to good teachers talk about their call to teach, the ideals that attract them, and the passions that sustain them, they almost always employ a rich moral and aesthetic vocabulary that is profoundly at odds with public discourse. Before reading further, we urge you to pause and recall what first attracted you to teaching. Seek those words within that allow you to give voice to your vocation. We believe it will open the door to an intuitive feeling for what it means to teach with reverence.

Many people think that they understand what reverence means, and so feel little need to contemplate further. However, we believe that at some level, reverence eludes definition. Reverence is primarily a vague and often inarticulable mood, and though it is not identical to awe and wonder, it commonly manifests itself in such primordial feelings. It is more an intuited feeling than an idea we can clearly comprehend. Unlike vague feelings, emotions have specific, definable objects (Damásio 2003). Primordially, reverence is not even a specific nameable emotion, although emotions like humility, shame, and respect may accompany it. The word "affectivity" derives from the Latin *affectus*, which means a state of openness that leaves us vulnerable to what is outside and beyond us, which attracts and moves us in many ways. It is not just passive "feeling." We will approach reverence through affectivity, although we will not restrict ourselves to the affective and active domain alone. Such moods, even when they give rise to more cognitively specifiable emotions, always splash over the categorical containers of discursive thought. We have found that it is best to approach the meaning of the word "reverence" through examples and descriptions in order to develop a fuller and richer understanding. That is why we asked that you consult your own intuitions before reading further.

Before trying to define the term, let us consider its affective quality in two commonplace depictions by teachers of teaching acts and occasions:

> Then I look them over and thought, *This is my destiny, to have this group of children before me. As they are growing, aging to be fifth graders, I was training, and now we meet, in this unique place and time.* The moment felt holy. (Codell 1999, 26, italics in the original)

Right at the entrance to Stephanie's room was a sign:

> Each child is sent into this world with
> a unique message to share...a new song
> to sing...a personal act of love to bestow.
> Welcome to Grade 1.
> I'm glad you're here. (Rose 1995, 107)

These statements show teachers expressing a strong sense of the sacred, of standing on hallowed ground, of destiny, of passion (and compassion), and of things toward which words may only point, but never hope to hold.

Let us see what we can learn when we examine these statements as also expressions of reverence.

Detecting reverence can be more a matter of moral and imaginative perception than cognition, although that too is important. It is more about being somebody than just knowing something; nonetheless, we need some definite idea about what we mean when we speak of reverence. Paul Woodruff gives a good capsule definition: Reverence is "the capacity for a range of feelings and emotions that are linked. It is a sense that there is something larger than a human being, accompanied by capacities for awe, respect, and shame; it is often expressed in, and reinforced by, ceremony" (2001, 63). Here is a more complete definition: Reverence is the comprehension of human limitation, imperfection, and our appropriate place in a community with others arising from feelings of awe and emotions of respect, shame, and humility regarding experiences of something or someone that meets at least one of the following conditions: (1) something or someone that cannot be changed or controlled by human means, something we are powerless to alter; (2) something or someone we cannot create; (3) something or someone we cannot completely understand; and (4) something or someone transcendent, something supernatural.

A few examples of "something" that meets one or more of these conditions are: the preciousness and frailty of life, justice, meaning and truth, ideas, ideals, love, death, nature, the creation, creativity, possibility, and human potential. Examples of "someone" include various notions of a Supreme Being, a hero or heroine, or an ordinary human whose capacity for noble acts exceeds the ordinary, such as Mahatma Gandhi, Reverend Martin Luther King Jr., or Mother Teresa. Then again, you may recall some of your teachers with a sense of gratitude that is somewhat akin to reverence.

While few of our authors work specifically with the above definition, most employ something resembling it, or parts of it, and all of them strive in different ways to capture the affective quality of reverence in teaching while issuing a call to intelligent action. We hope your own definition will grow as you read.

Consider the passage by Codell; we find that awe and wonder overcomes her. Many teachers feel something similar every year on the first day of class or, perhaps, on the last. For instance, after the concluding day of every class, one of us (A. G. Rud), says "goodbye" to the room that is now empty, sometimes uttering students' names and looking around and remembering who was there and what was discussed. He realizes that this class will never meet again and closes his eyes for a moment before turning off the lights and leaving. Many teachers express a profound sense of loss and grief at the end of the school year, and especially at graduation.

The Codell passage might meet all four conditions defined earlier. The "unique place and time" of her classroom encompasses a gathering of disparate ethnicities and nationalities. Besides those born in the United States, there are students in her fifth-grade class from Mexico, Pakistan, and the Philippines. The list of required supplies is given in English and Spanish. The events leading to this remarkable convergence of tongues and ethos lie beyond her control, as is the case with any educator. Teachers might admit a student or two and shift another out of their classroom, if they have the proper connections, but eventually they must accept the dappled multitude of human life that arrives in the seats before them. Many teachers have felt something overpowering in those gleaming, curious, and often confused eyes that confront them every day; there is something ultimately incomprehensible about any human being. At times, it can be frightening, but it can also fill the teacher with reverent awe, admiration, and wonder. As Codell writes, many times in the ensuing year, control of the class would slip out of her hands, sometimes into a teachable moment, sometimes into uncontrolled rage and violence. Codell, or "Madame Esmé" as she had the children call her, perceived the class as a gift, not something she created, although something she could creatively mold, if she is artist enough. Infinite human potential in a vibrant class of students, like the limitless possibilities of a blank canvas, can occasion reverence and conflict.

The greatest reverence lies beyond the power of words to capture. Codell feels that her first class on the first day of her career is holy; this might mean it is a spiritual experience, perhaps even the work of God. We do not at all wish to denigrate this reading of teaching as sometimes holy, and we believe reverent experience can and often should be religious, but we do want to note something. Woodruff writes: "Reverence has more to do with politics than religion" (2001, 4; see also 5). What he means is that reverence has more to do with the affairs of the *polis*, that is, literally the affairs of the city, the state, but most explicitly, communion within the community. Codell might have had a reverent experience of a community bound together by higher powers such as shared ideas and ideals that include the realization of human potential. We do not know, or need to know. Nor do we know or need to know exactly what reverence means. We do think that reverence for such things as truth, justice, or teaching can overcome profound differences in belief and value, including religious beliefs. Those that are reverent would never let mere ideological disagreement divide them before that mystery of existence that surely envelops something as beautiful and morally beneficial as caring, compassionate, competent, and wise teaching.

The sign posted at the entrance of Stephanie's classroom remarked on by Rose eludes full and sure understanding. One of the most powerful ideas in the entire history of the West is the Christian ideal of love as *agape*. Desire (*eros*) is possessive and friendship (*philia*) is conditional, but agape is a form of unconditional love given by the Creator. When it enters this material realm, it bestows value upon all who receive it regardless of their worth as usually judged. Ideally, agape should circulate in the community and return to its source uncorrupted. Even if one does not believe in the Creator, she or he may believe in the community within which agape flows. Each individual, including the teacher, in a learning community is a finite, needful being. Unconditional love allows individuals to satisfy their need to not only receive, but also give. In a healthy community, everyone deserves some respect and the showering of agape for private purposes will bring shame. Stephanie may well be seeking to extend God's love to all who enter her classroom, or she may just stand in reverent awe and wonder at every child's unique potential, destiny, and the exclusive song the children have to sing and personal acts of love they and she have to bestow. Either way, it is reverent.

Woodruff argues that reverence is a "cardinal virtue," that is, like courage, justice, or temperance we can find manifestations of it in many, though perhaps not all, cultures. Virtue ethics is concerned with the quality and content of our character. The organizing question of modern ethics has tended to be: "What are we morally obligated to do?" Answers to this question are usually "duty" ethics or "consequentialist" ethics. The organizing question of ancient ethics was usually: "What kind of person is it best to be?" The answer to this question is virtue ethics (Sher 1998, 1). Duty ethics along with ethical consequentialism (especially utilitarianism) dominates public morality in the modern age including public discourse surrounding teaching, at least in the West. Duty ethics places a strong emphasis on abstract, decontextualized moral rules, laws, obligations, and rights while utilitarianism emphasizes quantitative analysis to maximize the greatest good for the greatest number. Anyone familiar with educational bureaucracy understands how rules regulate and govern that sphere and how technocrats use numbers such as test scores and rankings to maximize perceived utility.

Virtue ethics concerns itself with attitudes, values, habits of action, imagination, feelings, interests, perceptions, and desires that serve as motives for human action. We are particularly interested in the feelings and emotions of awe, wonder, humility, shame, admiration, and respect associated with reverence. As Woodruff states, "Virtue ethics takes feelings seriously because feelings affect our lives more deeply than beliefs do...You may learn rules intellectually, and therefore you may learn or forget them very quickly" (2001, 6). Virtue concerns itself with the concrete particulars of specific situations and even one-time-only decision making.

Virtues cannot replace rules. A complete ethical theory includes following rules, knowing rights, carrying out duties, attending carefully to consequences, caring for others, and being concerned about the nature of the truly good. Virtuous persons, however, obey appropriate rules, carry out right action, and execute their social duties because of the constitution of their character as opposed to acting in response to external imposition or sheer force of inner will. Virtue involves moral perception. As teachers we cannot respond properly unless we can see clearly what needs doing in any unique situation with unique people (teachers, teacher aides, administrators, secretaries, students, lunch room personnel, parents, and many more). Virtue also involves moral imagination. We cannot act properly unless we can grasp all the possibilities of the situation that may be actualized. For instance, to teach well we must be able to grasp human potential or what Rose (1995) calls "possible lives."

The ethics of abstract and general rules, laws, and judgment may conflict with the concrete, sometimes one-time-only requirements of the ethics of care (compassion, connection, personal response) and the ethics of virtue. Teachers are members of a caring profession that is nonetheless obligated to the rules of the public or private bureaucratic institution wherein they may find themselves. In institutional settings, virtuous teachers must sometimes break rules to save children. The awe, wonder, humility, sense of shame, and respect that accompany the cardinal virtue of reverence provide restraint for those whose sense of care and calling carries them beyond the limits of bureaucratic rules and regulations. Reverence also requires that we sometimes break children or rather require them to conform to rules and regulations for the good of the larger order. Virtues often operate in the idiosyncratic gaps between rules, and when rules (or calculations) fail. They also help us apply rules correctly. Reverence contributes to the wisdom of teaching, which often lies beyond the bounds of good and evil as conventional morality defines it.

Virtue ethics appeals to emotions in ways the ethics of duty and of consequentialism do not. Besides the feeling of awe, wonder, and admiration, Woodruff examines three other emotions especially associated with reverence. They are respect, shame, and humility. Let us begin with respect and shame. Respect can be demonstrated through many forms, including the one we show for other people, a community, cultural traditions, social institutions, divine beings, and so on; we feel shame at our own failures and shortcomings regarding such objects of respect. Both are important to teaching. Shame and respect are intimately connected: "You cannot feel shame without feeling respect for something larger than yourself" (Woodruff 2001, 72). We are interested in the larger ideals and values of teaching such as reverence for the lives of students, actualizing students' full potential, dedication to self-transcending (though not self-eradicating) care and compassion for students, commitments to the truth of what we teach, and the communities we serve.

For those who live in the West and are more accustomed to guilt cultures, shame is harder to grasp than it is for those from the East. Whereas guilt tends to arise from a violation of one's internal values, which is further accompanied by regret and responsibility regarding some thought, feeling, or action, shame involves the whole person in regard to a violation of some deeply held social or cultural value. Hence, we may feel ashamed of thoughts, feelings, and actions unknown to others and guilty about things of which others approve. Shame is more about the whole person whereas guilt more often confines itself to some specific thought, feeling, or act. We may feel generally good about ourselves and guilty over some particular thing. Shame pervades the self.

Like any emotion, shame or guilt is good or bad depending on the situation and the values involved. Like reverence itself, we must always inquire into whether or not we should in fact feel shame at some of our actions. We should not let others shame us unquestioningly. Teachers who revere the ideals of their profession will feel shame when they fail to live their lives according to values common to all that share the calling. In reverent classrooms, teachers and students alike may feel shame when they fail the greater powers that unite the community.

The emotion of respect arises from reverence as naturally as the feelings of awe and wonder or the emotions of shame and humility. When the members of a community share reverence for something greater than any one of the individuals comprising the community, then they should show a degree of respect for every other member. For instance, we all share human life, are mortal, know love, joy, and sorrow, and we all hope and dream. Reverence for the human condition can unite us across vast differences of culture and religion. It may well be the supreme virtue of the multicultural classroom. Albert Schweitzer talked about reverence for life and the fellowship that bears the mark of suffering (Rud 2007; 2011). Surely, part of the human condition is that we all feel pain, suffer, and grieve; of course, we may also know peace and enduring life through our children and community contributions. Reverence for life must express care and compassion for suffering while seeking and celebrating joy, well-being, and peace. A teacher's reverence for life in the classroom will compassionately ameliorate anguish while seeking to bring about and celebrate joy. It helps connect teachers and students in their classroom as well as the school and larger community over generations.

Mutual respect in devotion to a shared ideal may bind people together even when it is obvious that some should be held in much higher esteem than others because of their superior wisdom, moral character, or ability. All are equally humbled before the might of the mystery. Even criminals or classroom mischief-makers deserve a modicum of respect when it is time to distribute justice. That is why we should ameliorate the severity of our judgment when the transgressor is truly contrite. Just laws, conjoined with the capacity for caring compassionately—and forgiving (even forgetting) when necessary—can transcend a good deal for the greater good.

Classroom discipline should be reverent; it should never be an ego struggle between the teacher and the student. Those who work with the young know that children keenly value justice and fair play. Teachers must show special respect for the ignorant; they should realize that only education can give the ignorant a better understanding. In the classroom community, it is possible for all to share reverence for learning, the quest for meaning, and the ideals of human flourishing along with reverence for life, even though a few realize the importance of these better than others. After all, overcoming ignorance, including our own ignorance and insensitivity, is the central task of teaching.

Teachers may surpass students in knowledge and wisdom, yet all are due respect. Teaching is a knowing and caring profession wherein we must be willing to acknowledge occasions when our students know more, practice compassion better, and even display greater wisdom than we. Everyone stands to learn something from one another in a truly reverent classroom. However much they may know, it is but a drop in an endless ocean. Reverent teachers will acknowledge their own limitations in emotion, deed, and, deliberation while remaining respectful of the limitations of others. They should be especially diligent at detecting imposters that falsely attempt to capture their reverent sensibilities.

Woodruff calls attention to "imposter virtues," which he defines as "ideas that make us feel good about doing bad things" (2001, 70). He comments: "Imposter virtues generally cloud the mind" (ibid., 71). Those who believe that human customs are the will of God can too easily follow a false prophet just as free peoples fail in their democratic duty when they do not question their country's leaders, and open the way for tyranny even as they think they are defending democracy. Woodruff suggests we can avoid imposter virtues by never suspending "our own moral judgment or closing the lid on our own moral compasses" (ibid., 72). We agree with Woodruff when he insists: "Reverence sets a higher value on the truth than on any human product that is supposed to have captured the truth" (ibid., 39). We also concur when he suggests that reverence "cherishes freedom of inquiry" (ibid.). It requires that we respect such things as a school's tradition, its teacher, its leadership, the larger community, and the value of educating young people—a principle that almost everyone shares—but it requires more from us than just that. We must also critically examine our tradition, teaching, leadership, community, and values, including our individual values, and when necessary, imaginatively recreate them. Reverence for reflection, truth, and inquiry is always higher than reverence for a dogmatic assertion of truth.

Reverence supports freedom of inquiry, which is the first thing tyranny suppresses. Truth can most inspire reverential attitudes when we realize that it transcends the human condition. Finite creatures are not and never will be omniscient. Recognition of human limitation humbles all before the mystery of the unknown and, perhaps, unknowable. Truth can never be the possession of only one person or one leader, however wise. The quest for truth and understanding belongs to every member of the community who answers the call, including those who have come before and those who are yet to come. Many teachers are not learners. Reverent teachers are open to learning because they know they are vulnerable to the shifting contingencies of existence and recognize that even the most assured position is subject to refutation. Reverence for truth alerts teachers to the permanent possibility of error. Good teaching requires intelligent inquiry into both the practice of teaching and the subject content of what we teach.

Irreverence means showing a lack of respect for something or someone. Reverence is a virtue, but, sometimes, irreverence is required. If, upon careful reflection, something the community commends as worthy of universal reverence proves undeserving, we need not act reverently toward it. Sometimes, irreverence is the proper attitude; indeed, sometimes it is what true reverence requires. However, in our times, there seems to be a tendency to mock even the highest and the best, and not the undeserving. Irreverence becomes the greatest folly when we mock the grandest values of the community without proper warrant. Such irreverence destroys individuals and communities because it corrupts virtuous action. We do not respect others in our community and fail to feel shame when we realize we should have given respect. When irreverence overcomes everything of worth, we have entered an era of nihilism that destroys all meanings and values human or transcendent.

We began by probing the meaning of the term reverence; however, we do not think we have come anywhere close to an exhaustive understanding. The chapters that follow each explores various facets of reverence, but leaves many others unexamined, perhaps even unrecognized. The chapters consider those aspects of reverence we have mentioned already such as incomprehensibility, uncontrollability, the transcendent, human limitation, awe, wonder, shame, respect, admiration, as well as others we have not mentioned such as patience, curiosity, silence, infinite possibility, and receptiveness to gifts.

As you read, we urge you to constantly inquire into what you find. Do you agree, or disagree? What is missing? How do you feel about what you have read? Have your own thought and intuitions changed since we asked you to pause, listen to yourself, and give voice to your vocation? What, if anything, should you do differently based on these readings?

Robert Boostrom poses a remarkable question to contemporary educational reformers. Suppose we achieved the aims of high test scores, every student was at "grade level" and there was universal high-school graduation. Would we be truly happy? Bob does not think so. These are not ends-in-themselves. Boostrom suggests that "the practice of reverent teaching is, I believe, the true love we overlook." For him, the practice of reverent teaching seeks to "nurture" what, borrowing from Emerson, he calls the "greater possibility," "the seeds of growth," in other human beings. However, that means "nurturing an unknown." This requires faith, and reverence, "an *admiring* wonder" for the unknown and perhaps unknowable in our students. Teachers are much more than "knowledge" workers refining human resources for the global production function.

Bob focuses on five dimensions of reverent teaching. The first is a form of self-transcendent listening that sets aside our purposes and lives in hope that others will reveal themselves to us in ways that allow us perceive, and perhaps help them realize, their best possibilities. The second is "thinking" that "is the call of reverence to action." Reverence that does not involve dispositions for action is merely sentimentality. Reverence concerns the content of our character. Thoughtful action in teaching is responsive to others and includes imagination, feelings, and discerning perception along with discursive acumen, but that is not all. The third dimension "is social, or interdependent thinking." We should remember that the word "logic" derives from the ancient Greek *logos*, which, among many other things, means discourse. The logical is always dialogical. A soliloquy is a flawed, fragmented, and incomplete thought. Listening is critical to logical thinking properly understood; it is also critical to "logical" teaching. Then again, so is his fourth dimension, laughter. Reverence need not always be somber. As Bob observes, "Laughter expresses the humility of reverence." Human limitation and imperfection has long been an essence of comedy. "So, the laughter of the reverent teacher is in part the nervous laugh of self-awareness, and embarrassed recognition of one's own limitations," but as he goes on to point out, "it is also a laugh of playfulness." Playfulness is a perfectly reverent pedagogical response to that we cannot create, control, or completely understand. So too is Bob's last dimension: love. If anything lies beyond our complete comprehension and control and yet deserves our highest reverence, this is it. Teaching is a caring profession. When the caring goes beyond unconditional love and acceptance of the infinite possibilities of others in relation to the infinite possibility of the subject matter, and beyond the bounds of complete control and comprehension, it becomes something we cannot create, but that we may reverently receive as a transcendent gift. Finally, and unexpectedly, reverent teachers "correct" their students. This is not just the usual formative evaluation, although that too has its place in reverent teaching and correction. Rather, "when a reverent teacher believes that a student is moving away from the greater possibility, she must correct." In reverent teaching, commonplace correction emerges out of a reverent grasp of greater possibilities.

Daniel P. Liston weaves a wonderful web of connections among reverence, the reverential classroom, and the intricacies of what he calls "attentive love." We must reverently recognize our human limitation in understanding our students. This is especially so when their life narratives are vastly different from those with which we are familiar. In awe and wonder, we must simply accept that we can never completely comprehend others. This insight brings a sense of respect for others and a sense of shame when we fail to honor them and their differences.

However, Dan believes, the reverential classroom ethos is one in which attentive love is practiced such that we may strive to understand one another better and more justly, however imperfectly. The reverential classroom also involves awe and wonder for beauty in the search for enduring meaning and truth exemplified by passionate teachers who desire to connect their students to the subject matter through a shared inquiry in which all are humbled before the mystery of the topics' infinite possibilities.

Attentive love assumes that actual and potential good exists within each of our students. Such love seeks to discern this goodness however concealed. It involves teachers reaching beyond themselves for not only what is good in others, but also what is worthy in the social, cultural, and natural worlds we share. Through sharing beauty and a common inquiry into the good and true of some subject matter larger than any one of us, we may come to appreciate each other across vast differences. Teachers may also exercise moral perception that seeks the meaning of the particular details, the mannerisms, interests, dress, and enthrallments, of our students. Finally, in order to do all this, we must quiet the noise of ourselves. We must eclipse for a time our own needs, desires, beliefs, values, and purposes and perhaps even see ourselves from the uncomplimentary perspective of others.

Michael Dale shows how we may seek reverence in teaching by way of silence even though the ethos of schools and schooling, including teacher education, actually work against silence, and thereby reverence. However, for any relation between student, teacher, and subject matter to yield a truly reverent classroom, we must somehow find a way to sometimes quell the noise and busyness of our work, and our lives.

Michael helps us see how noisy our lives are. How everyone in the school in community is obsessed with "getting"; getting information, getting the right answer, getting a degree, getting through, producing, and achieving. He explains how utilitarian, calculative rationality has taken over our lives and how narrow, instrumentalist means-ends reasoning requires us to accept assigned ends unreflectively, and only think about the means of getting them. The idea is to master, control, use, and consume as quickly as possible. Our entire culture has become obsessed with having more rather than being more, which is where reverence might enter. No wonder such busyness dominates the field of education. What we want most from our students, we cannot take from them, however good our teaching technique. It is theirs to give. Michael reminds us that reverence, like the scent of the rose, "is a gift you receive with gratitude."

Michael would help us seek gifts by way of silence rather than linear logic. He urges us to engage our calling and our students noninstrumentally and he helps us to name the absent in our lives. He begins by urging careful reflection and contemplation, which he carefully distinguishes. Reflection, he indicates, involves a "bending back" upon ourselves while contemplation directs itself toward the other. Reverence is less about reflection than contemplation, although both require silencing the noise within and without. In reverence, we are seized by something beyond us, something beyond our understanding and control, something far beyond utilitarian calculation. Perhaps we listen with the kind of attentive love described in Daniel Liston's chapter. In any case, it involves the virtue of humility.

Sam M. Intrator explores reverence through the experience of epiphanies within the course of a teaching life. Epiphany involves intuitive leaps of understanding, insight, even revelation wherein the greater meaning of some, often mundane, experience suddenly discloses itself. Such experiences readily evoke a sense of reverence. Certainly grasping the fuller meaning, truth, and possibility within the subject matter we teach may evoke reverence, especially when we share it with others in the class.

Early in the chapter we meet a thirty-five-plus year veteran Brooklyn teacher whose most intense memory is of a lesson on the Gettysburg Address he gave every year. He remembers powerful emotions in the room in the lines that invoked a shared sense of the "miracle" of America to the kids from so many different lands: "that this nation, under God, shall have a new birth of freedom—and that government of the people, by the people, for the people, shall not perish from the earth." Here we have shared reverence for something, the United States of America, at an extraordinarily vulnerable moment in its history. We also have reverence for the ideals of justice and a better life for which it stands. There is also a clear presence of something or someone transcendent or supernatural. It readily evokes humility and mutual respect before something that the class did not create, cannot entirely control, nor fully understand, although it is something to which they might contribute with patriotic love, provided, of course, that they carry out the appropriate inquiry to make sure they are not falling for an imposter that would lead to tyranny. Reverence resides within every epiphanic "spots of time that glow" like this vignette Sam documents through his research and discusses in his chapter.

Carol Rodgers recounts and discusses the reverence she finds in a teacher's (Annie) capacity to perceive with profound insight, or, what we earlier called moral and imaginative perception. Moreover, she finds the same reverent perception in the practices of the entire school where Annie interned. Like any other virtue, we cannot effectively teach reverence entirely didactically; however, we can absorb it by participating in the customary practices of a reverent community. Carol makes an immensely important distinction between genuine, insightful perception and mere recognition for the purposes of ready naming and identification.

One powerful metaphor for reverence in teaching is what David Hansen (2004) calls a "poetics of teaching." Carol writes, "where the teacher is moved by and responsive to the expressiveness of the child's commerce with the world." Good poetry operates at the very limits of language and can gesture beyond those limits toward what we sometimes cannot name or know. It can capture the feelings of awe, wonder, and admiration associated with reverent teaching. A poetics of teaching addresses the aesthetic, moral, and intellectual dimensions of teaching together in reticulated ways. It examines teaching as a creative meaning-making activity some components of which, like poetry itself, work beyond the limits of language, interpretation, and recognition.

Elaine J. O'Quinn's chapter is a pastiche, a medley of teaching moments and memories that invoke our often inarticulate feelings and unsure emotions, and call us again to reverence the mystery of teaching. As you read her chapter, we urge you to recall your own moments of reverent teaching—or learning. How did it feel then, how does it feel now? Why do we still carry them with us? Do we possess these memories, or do they possess us? This simple exercise offers one way of releasing reverence within our lives and our teaching as well as the lives of our students.

If Woodruff is right that reverence has more to do with politics than religion, Elaine reminds us that the private is often public within classroom communities. In the reverent classroom, we experience many communal moments when we cannot hide ourselves from others, or they from us. Elaine recognizes the risk and vulnerability that accompany the reverent recognition that our students and their lives are often incomprehensible and uncontrollable. She shows that sometimes we must simply be willing to rely on, and receive, grace.

As the title of his contribution suggests, William H. Schubert looks carefully at the objects of putative reverence. He does so in terms of his own personal, evolving, teaching narrative. In so doing, he provides a helpful example of the kind of critical-creative inquiry we urge our readers to engage in for themselves regarding the meaning of reverence in their teaching lives. Some of the objects include reverence for "sanctioned authority" as expressed by "Grandpa Schubert," such cultural constructions as "basketball and fundamentalist religion," the "liberal arts and great ideas," "progressive theory and practice," "student interests," "teacher learning," "engaging in the quest with students and others," and "the quest" itself. There is even a rumination "beyond objects of reverence" that includes worries about where the objects of reverence reside. It leads to conjectures about "reverence for connection, for wholeness." Acknowledging that "the idea of appeal to authority doubtless remained encoded in my educational pursuits," the results of his inquiry reside far from the authoritarian. Bill's journey testifies that we cannot grow without loss.

William Ayers opens his chapter with a reference to the Puerto Rican poet Judith Ortiz Cofer that the lesson teachers should teach is to sing. Bill's chapter is a prophetic cry. It is not Mosaic prophecy like Moses' foretelling the future of his people, but a statement of things true in all times and places where "engaged teachers" believe that "each student is unique, each the one and only who will ever trod the earth, each worthy of a certain reverence." At times it has the tincture of the anger of the Hebrew prophets. It is also a lament for an age in which the "ingredients for reverence are quashed and sacrificed." In other ways, it is also a plea, a testament to democratic community in desperate times. Perhaps it is even some kind of humanistic prayer. He uses the kind of moral and aesthetic vocabulary entirely missing from the contemporary dialogue about teaching and learning noted earlier. Bill's contribution expresses well the elusiveness that surrounds the very idea of reverence. Whatever you may think about his chapter, our introduction, or any other chapter in this volume, we urge you explore it for your own unique reverent purposes since it is our hope that we have gathered for you a community of fellow inquirers. For, as Bill remarks, "Regard extends, importantly, to the larger community—the wide, wide world that animates each individual life."

In her chapter, Megan J. Laverty explores reverence through the experience of the sublime. Such experience occurs at the point of intelligent comprehension of any kind as we intuit a deeply felt transcendent, nonrepresentable reality. She focuses first on Immanuel Kant's construction of the sublime in terms of an awakening to Reason through the failure of Understanding and Imagination that humbles the empirical self by confrontation with the overwhelmingly powerful forces of existence. For Kant, such experience prompts us to pursue the moral life in terms of what is higher and completely pure (i.e., acting from duty) as opposed to the base empirical motives. However, Megan prefers Iris Murdoch's correction of the self-directed, lonely defiance in Kant's free exercise of Reason. Murdoch does not think Reason can command the reverent feeling of the sublime, nor can it uniquely inspire such experience. Murdoch primarily criticizes Kant for his fear of the messiness, incompleteness, and historicity of empirical particulars; for instance, particularly people such as teachers and students. Megan concludes with concrete suggestions for fostering contemplation and conversation by acknowledging with Simone Weil that while our intelligence cannot penetrate the mystery, the words we use to describe it remain immensely important. Therefore, she thinks it is vital to have students learn to carefully describe the world in detail rather than just write and talk about it as an abstract and discrete subject. Teachers might ask their students, and expect of themselves, to learn to write and talk in such a way as to meticulously depict what they experience. The chapter opens with her own painstaking depiction of the Korean film *Poetry*. Megan thereby provides the reader with a wonderful example of what she is urging us to do as well.

Bruce Novak ends the volume with a note of hope by developing what he calls mediated reverence. He explores the psychological processes that enable us to "understand both how art teaches and how a certain kind of artistry lies at the heart of teaching." Bruce shows us how we can share our lives in what Whitman called a "sublime and serious *Religious Democracy*" where our lives are enmeshed together and art provides us with connection to show how we revere, hold in awe and wonder, the lives we have together. But that is not all, since such artistry not only shares, but also is generative. That is what happens in teaching and in art when this kind of generative sharing occurs, as Novak describes in relation to an exercise in writing poetry that he asks readers to do:

> For *new* life has been evoked by their temporary sharing of life, as you yourself experienced in the writing of your poem, if this exercise worked for you. And it is the miraculousness of this new life that is particularly deserving of reverence: the fact that new life has been created from a set of

black spots on a white page, and that through this transubstantiation, life itself has vibrantly kept on going, has blossomed anew.

Novak does not see this as an easy task, but something profoundly worthwhile. He asks us to imagine what teaching would be like if teachers were taught rigorously but with the aim to put that rigor in the service of cultivating talent and an appreciation and reverence for the wonders of life. Novak's vision of "a democracy in which the virtue of reverentially recognizing and learning from the gifts of others has become a fundamental habit of everyday life" is a society where the virtue of reverence has been revived and reestablished, and where the words of our authors are not foreign to how we live together.

References

Codell, E. R. 1999. *Educating Esmé: Diary of a Teacher's First Year*. Chapel Hill, NC: Algonquin Books.
Damásio, A. 2003. *Looking for Spinoza: Joy, Sorrow and the Feeling Brain*. London: William Heinemann.
Rose, M. 1995. *Possible Lives: The Promise of Public Education in America*. New York: Penguin Books.
Rud, A. G. 2007. "Caring for Others as a Path to Teaching and Learning: Albert Schweitzer's Reverence for Life." In *Ethical Visions of Education: Philosophies in Practice*. Edited by D. T. Hansen, 157–171. New York: Teachers College Press.
———. 2011. *Albert Schweitzer's Legacy for Education: Reverence for Life*. New York: Palgrave Macmillan.
Rud, A. G., and J. Garrison, 2010. "Reverence and Listening in Teaching and Leading." *Teachers College Record* 112 (11): 2777–2792.
Sher, G. 1998. "Ethics, Character, and Action." In *Virtue and Vice*. Edited by E. Frankel, F. Miller, and J. Paul, 1–17. Cambridge: Cambridge University Press.
Woodruff, P. 2001. *Reverence: Renewing a Forgotten Virtue*. New York: Oxford University Press.

1

The Practice of Reverent Teaching

Robert Boostrom

All too often we find ourselves—if we are honest—behaving like Scarlett O'Hara pining for Ashley Wilkes. We chase around in futility after one thing, when something else that would satisfy our aching need is right in front of us. Another story (made into a movie just a few years after *Gone with the Wind*) reveals the insight even more pointedly: in *Random Harvest* an amnesiac seeks the love of a forgotten life only to discover that he is married to her.

Educational reform is plagued by a similar amnesia. We ought to ask ourselves what would happen if current educational aims—children reading at "grade level," students and schools meeting test-score goals, universal high school graduation, college enrollments and completion rates rising—were actually met. Would we enter a golden age? Would terrorism end and the religious and political leaders of the world embrace each other? Would economic success, civility, and political wisdom be ours? Would our children become the people we hoped they'd be? Or would we merely discover that achieving our current educational aims would never, after all, make us truly happy?

In the realm of educational aims, the practice of reverent teaching is, I believe, the true love we overlook. But what do I mean with this sentimental-sounding metaphor? What is reverent teaching?

I am thinking of reverence as the consciousness of a finite being in an infinite universe. We are jolted by the realization that somehow we know that we don't know, somehow we see what is beyond our reach, because even in our limited state we participate in the infinite. We feel "a kind of latent omniscience not only in every man, but in every particle" (Emerson

1929, 1001). We believe—especially we teachers—that every person has a greater possibility:

> Every man supposes himself not to be fully understood; and if there is any truth in him, if he rests at last on the divine soul, I see not how it can be otherwise. The last chamber, the last closet, he must feel was never opened; there is always a residuum unknown, unanalyzable. That is, every man believes he has a greater possibility. (Ibid., 217)

We all have within us seeds of growth. To teach is to nurture that growth in others, but this means nurturing an unknown. The greater possibility calls for the teacher to have faith in that which has not yet been proven, and may never be proved. Reverence is the combination of our awareness of the mystery of the "greater possibility" together with our response of admiring wonder:

> In other words, what sets men wondering is something familiar and yet normally invisible, and something men are forced to *admire*. The wonder that is the starting-point of thinking is neither puzzlement nor surprise nor perplexity; it is an *admiring* wonder. (Arendt 1971, 143)

The teacher who is struck by admiring wonder at her student's greater possibility has begun the act of reverent teaching. At least, she has a reverent frame of mind. The problem is to carry that reverence into action. Teachers cannot simply sit in awe in the face of their students' inexhaustible potential; teachers must evaluate and judge and correct. They must, sometimes, act in ways that will hurt those they revere. So, how can admiring wonder at the students' greater possibility be carried into teaching practice?

To answer this question I offer five dimensions of reverent teaching, five ways in which teachers interact with students—listen, think, laugh, love, and correct. Together, they portray what I mean when I speak of the practice of reverent teaching.

Listen

Listening is the openness of reverence. It is the willingness to feel awe. When we listen, we set aside our purposes, and put our self in the hands of another. Listening, says John Dewey, implies passivity and dependence (1976, 22). Yes, and it also implies expectation. We listen *for* something or *to* something because we have hope of revelation.

Without listening, teaching dies before it is born. Some years ago, I taught a high school English class in which I had one especially disengaged student. She did nothing in class. She turned in no homework, she participated in no discussions, and she failed all tests. At the end of the semester, when exam week came, I was astonished to see her. Students were to come to school only if they had an exam scheduled, and while there was an exam in the class, I was sure the student must have realized she would fail the course regardless of her exam grade. Besides, how could she suppose that she would pass an exam when she had failed every test in the class?

That final meeting was the first time that I understood that I had not been listening to her. Having concluded at almost the beginning of the semester that she intended to fail, I had not believed in her greater possibility.

When I write about my failure to listen to this student, I am not talking only, or even especially, about language. Yes, it's true that when we link the words *listen* and *teacher*, there will be a tendency to think of the teacher listening to the words that students say. When we think about teachers listening to students, we tend to focus on the verbal evidence that conforms to our expectations of instruction. For instance, teachers listen for wrong answers to questions—evidence that students are not paying attention or that they do not understand the material. Wrong answers are useful because they give a teacher something to do: she corrects the mistakes, or she chastises students for not following along, or she reviews or elaborates on the material.

But this "listening to the words that students say" too easily becomes a peculiar way of not listening at all. We begin with a good impulse—perhaps we call it "finding out where students are"—and, in keeping with the accountability-through-assessment craze, reduce "finding out where students are" to mean using some sort of pretest and posttest to determine what number can be given to each student on a unidimensional scale of achievement. We act as if students exist only on this scale of school-prescribed curricular outcomes, forgetting that they exist also, and more importantly, in their friendships, their longings, their love of music, their playfulness, their fears, their losses, their disappointments, their heroes, and their inborn desire (as Aristotle put it) to know.

When I use the word *listen* to write about this broad attention to the lives of students—this reverence for their greater possibility—it may seem that I have chosen the wrong word. I am obviously speaking about a kind of attentiveness that differs from the sort of listening that requires only the registry of aural input. In the classroom, it might be said, attentiveness is better characterized by the word *watch*, a word more likely to suggest the "withitness" (Kounin 1970) of a teacher who is sensitive to students' needs, the "sympathetic" teacher Dewey writes of (1976, 89–90) who knows what students want before they know themselves. But watchful withitness is really the antithesis of the sort of listening I have in mind when I talk about the openness of reverence. The teacher who is reverent is not out ahead of events; she is instead caught in an unfolding moment.

The two activities—watchful withitness and reverent listening—may, of course, overlap, as the following scene illustrates:

> [Ms. Hamilton] continued to work with [the reading group] the Lollipops. On the board she'd written *mad*, and she asked one of the Lollipops to read it. Then she wrote *bad* and asked a different child to read that. Then she wrote *had* and asked Felicia to read it. Felicia was stumped.
>
> "Okay," said Ms. Hamilton, pointing to *bad* and *had*, "what's the same about these two words? What's different about them?" Felicia was just figuring it out when Ms. Hamilton noted that Richard (who was at the far end of the room from her) was talking rather loudly to the girl at the desk closest to him. He'd been talking to her about picking out a pumpkin for Halloween.
>
> "Richard! Richard!" said Ms. Hamilton, "are you visiting or helping?" Without a pause, Richard said, "Helping."
>
> "Could you do it in a quieter voice?" (Jackson et al. 1993, 54)

Seemingly absorbed in helping Felicia (and keeping the reading group lesson moving along), Ms. Hamilton is simultaneously watchful of the children in the rest of the room. She responds to Richard's chatter with a question that shows her shaping the situation: she is in control; she exemplifies withitness.

But Ms. Hamilton's response to Richard illustrates a shift to a different kind of listening. Rather than simply telling Richard to be quiet, she asks a question that denies she is in control. Her question—"Are you visiting or helping?"—announces to all the children in the classroom that Richard, not she, will classify what he is doing. Her second question—"Could you do it in a quieter voice?"—verifies that she accepts his classification.

Now, when Ms. Hamilton asks these questions, what is she listening to? I struggle with this simple matter because I realize that what I just said about Ms. Hamilton's questions may misrepresent what happened. When Ms. Hamilton asks Richard, "Are you visiting or helping?" she knows what he will say. She has framed the question in a manner that forces the choice upon him because everyone in the room knows that "visiting" goes against the rules, but "helping" is all right. Of course, Richard will say he is helping. He may be the one who officially classifies his activity, but she has given him the categories and practically forced one on him. Ms. Hamilton is ostensibly asking for a classification, but she not only knows the classification, she's actually provided it. The interaction is more like the enactment of a tiny drama than a genuine exchange of information. Ironically, it is only within the context of the drama (written by the teacher) that the teacher denies she is in control.

So, is Ms. Hamilton listening at all? Or is she just telling Richard to stop talking? Where is the openness of reverence?

Suppose we imagine the listening of a reverent teacher as something comparable to the way we listen to music. While it is often said that music conveys no information or content (in the way that language does), most of us feel that when we listen to music, something happens to us, often something quite profound.

But this may not be true for everyone. Those who suffer with amusia are incapable of hearing music (Sacks 2008, 105–128). They can hear the sounds that a violin or a piano makes, they can hear a choir vocalizing, and some (not all with amusia) can tell the difference between a flute and a trombone, perhaps even the difference between one note and another. But those who suffer with amusia cannot hear *music*, and their disability helps reveal something remarkable about the rest of us.

Most of us human beings have the capacity to hear sounds not as noise (meaningless aural input) but as music (meaningful nonlinguistic communication). Some have argued that this capacity to hear music is a major factor in the evolutionary development of humankind. "The social complexity of the early hominids and Early Humans," writes Steven Mithen (2006, 147), "created selective pressures for enhanced communication." The ability to create and to hear music provided, even before the development of language, Mithen argues, "the type of subtle and sensitive communication that is required for the development and maintenance of social relationships" (ibid., 148). Making and hearing music served, he suggests, as a kind of social grooming that, unlike picking nits out of someone else's fur, could be accomplished over a distance or while on the move. To listen to the vocalizing of another member of the group—to hear it as music—is to feel the presence of that person. A mother sings to her infant, and the music expresses her desire to keep the child warm and fed and safe from harm.

Martha Nussbaum discusses this power of music in her study of emotion—*Upheavals of Thought*. She quotes Marcel Proust, who seems to foreshadow Mithen's argument for the role of music in human development and life. "I wondered," says Proust (quoted in Nussbaum 2001, 266), "whether music might not be the unique example of what might have been—if the invention of language, the formation of words, the analysis of ideas had not intervened—the means of communication between souls."

This listening that connects souls is reverent listening, and while I don't suggest that Ms. Hamilton and Richard are making beautiful music, it does seem to me that their vocalizing has more to do with connection than with content. On both sides there are acknowledgement and assurance, and there is the listening that signifies the openness of reverence.

Think

Thinking is the call of reverence to action. It is the sharing of reverence—a sharing that rejects the metaphor of teaching by pouring in.

John Dewey famously asked, "Why is it that teaching by pouring in, learning by passive absorption, are universally condemned, yet entrenched in practice?" (1980, 43). It is a profound question, but his answer—that the dictum is preached instead of practiced—is, unfortunately, no answer at all. To say that we preach because we have to preach doesn't add much to our understanding.

If it can be said that there is any single or primary reason that "teaching by pouring in" remains the teacher's dominant mode, it is, I suspect, that thinking is too great a mystery. What I have in mind begins where listening left off. Why is it so hard to listen? Because it seems so necessary to talk. The hardest thing for any teacher to do (especially a novice teacher) is to do nothing in class. The easiest thing to do is to talk, to fill the supposedly empty space with sound. The admonition to listen challenges us because it implies that silence is not the same as emptiness, and this is a hard lesson to learn, especially hard with the enormous pressure on teachers for data-driven assessment results. The craze for accountability-through-assessment loudly insists that every classroom moment be filled with either the sound of prescribed instruction or the demonstration of student mastery.

So, as teachers, we fear silence because we believe that nothing comes from nothing, that we cannot pull something from students until we pour something into them, that we cannot expect them to think about something until we have given them something to think about. The Socratic answer to this fear was, of course, a myth of reincarnation and a theory of learning-as-recollection. If knowledge lies forgotten within us (as Socrates argues in *Meno* [Plato 1997, 81 b–d]), then questions can bring forth knowing from silence; it will seem as if something comes from nothing. And here, in this something—from-nothing, is the source of Hannah Arendt's "wonder that is the starting-point of thinking," for all thinking has something of the magical—something "out of thin air"—about it. Here is an example of what I mean:

> Some years ago I sat in a second-grade classroom, observing the children at work. One of the girls was sitting at a desk near me, solving some arithmetic problems, and after a while she approached me for help.

"I can't get this one," she said.

I read the problem, which said something like this: "Godzilla was smashing houses in Tokyo. He smashed seven houses with his right foot and eight houses with his left foot. How many houses did he smash all together?"

The problem didn't seem to me to be all that difficult for this second-grade class. The children had been adding one-digit numbers for some time, so I wondered why this question stumped the girl. I thought that perhaps she was unable to read the question, so I asked her to read it to me, which she did without any stumbling, hesitating, or misreading.

More puzzled than before, I made some conversation while I pondered how to help the girl. "Do you know who Godzilla is?" I asked.

"No."

"He's a monster in a lot of Japanese movies." I went on to describe from as best I could recall the appearance of Godzilla (sort of a fire-breathing tyrannosaurus) and to mention some of his more notable battles. I dimly remembered that Godzilla defeated King Kong and an assortment of other monsters that threatened Earth (repeatedly). I think I said something about primitive special effects and about awkward dubbing from Japanese into English. Eventually, the girl looked up at me and said, "OK, I've got it," and she went back to her seat and solved the arithmetic problem. (Boostrom 2005, 80)

I offer this story because it remains for me an "open work," a story that "invites further reflection and commentary" (Jackson et al. 1993, 49). Even now, after having revisited the scene many times in the past twenty years, I do not feel that I fully understand what happened. But the story illustrates several aspects of what I have in mind when I talk about the thinking that is part of reverent teaching.

First, this is (on my part, certainly) tentative thinking, populated with uncertainty and hypothetical conjectures. It is not the application of principles or the accurate following of procedure or algorithm. In fact, it is closer to stumbling than it is to knowing. Why did I choose to ask the girl about a character in the word problem rather than to talk with her about addition? Other than to say, "It seemed like a good idea at the time," I don't know. I am certain that I deliberately avoided telling her the answer to the arithmetic problem (because I still avoid telling students answers), but that predisposition didn't necessarily lead me to reminisce on Godzilla.

Second, this is descriptive (rather than prescriptive) thinking, but at the same time it is practical (rather than theoretical) thinking. My thinking, as I encountered this student, did not grow out of, or lead to, any generalizations about how to teach arithmetic. I was as narrowly focused on the problem at hand as was the student, but the immediate problem at hand, for me, was to understand what the girl was asking me, not to determine an appropriate instructional intervention. Asking, "Do you know who Godzilla is?" becomes an instructional hypothesis (something like, "perhaps this lacuna in her reading of the problem is interfering with her ability to add the numbers") only because the girl goes on to solve the problem.

Third, this is social, or interdependent, thinking. I can write (as I just did) about "my thinking," but neither my thinking nor hers is separate from the encounter. The girl initiated the "remediation," and my question, "Do you know who Godzilla is?" is a response to what she initiated. We are thinking together; we are sharing the reverence.

Another story from my own teaching may help to bring into clearer focus the tentative, descriptive, and social characteristics of reverent thinking, because in this second story my thinking does not have these characteristics. This time the class is an undergraduate course in educational history and philosophy, and I had asked the students to read Galway Kinnell's poem, "The Schoolhouse." Preparing for class, I looked through the poem for those passages and references I thought might create difficulties for the students. I was consciously looking for what I called (remembering the story from the second-grade classroom) "Godzillas." I would need, I told myself, to talk about Socrates and Diotima, about Troilus and Cressida, about Otway and Chatterton, about the Garden of Eden and the Tree of Knowledge and death, about "innocents who sponge periodicals," about "fighting in Latin the wars of the Greeks," about the funeral oration of Pericles, and about constellations and the big bang. I was excited by the delightful mix of these various elements all brought together in one poem reflecting on the significance of schooling and of a teacher. And I patted myself on the back for offering students such a rich experience. My thinking was certain, prescriptive, and private.

My plan was to read the poem aloud, then to discuss the elements I had selected (plus addressing any questions the students raised), and finish by reading the poem aloud again. The plan went off—it seemed to me—without a hitch, until, after I had finished my thoughtful elucidations of the text, one student raised her hand. She said, "I don't understand where they say, 'We are the school of Hellas.'"

I was a little disappointed, since I had explained that the line came from the funeral oration of Pericles, and I had given some of the context of the speech and some background on Pericles. But I went back to that material, and this time I added more about the role of Athens in the history of Greece in the fifth century BC. As I spoke, I watched the student's face for some sign of acknowledgment that I had satisfied her inquiry. It didn't come.

When I finished, I looked to her, inviting comment if she had any, and she said, "I get that, but what does *Hellas* mean?"

Now, readers may say to themselves, "I knew what the student's problem was as soon as she asked the question. How could you not know that she didn't understand the word *Hellas*? What were you thinking?" But, of course, that's exactly my point.

My thinking may have been informed, reflective, insightful, and spirited; but it was not reverent. Setting out to deal with the unavoidable educational problem of "Godzillas," I had tried to think without listening, and I had wasted both my time and their time. I had not been thinking about, or with, the students at all.

My motives in this second story are, I hope, understandable. I wanted to help the students. I believed that they could find insight in Kinnell's poem. "We all stand waiting," writes Emerson [1929, 219], "empty—knowing, possibly, that we can be full, surrounded by mighty symbols that are not symbols to us, but prose and trivial toys." And I would, I told myself, help my students to become full; I would help them feel the power of the "mighty symbols." I would show them how they could share in my reverence. But this is pride talking, not reverence. This is me mistakenly believing (or wishfully hoping) that with the eloquence of my words and the music of my voice, I could pour insight and reverence into my students.

Laugh

Laughter expresses the humility of reverence. We who are teachers know that there is a dark joke in teaching because teaching is always a kind of failing. Whatever we accomplish, we always leave some things undone: while our lofty aims reach out to the unknown possibilities of untold generations, they can only be enacted through the trivial everyday life of schools. Billy Collins captures the mundane absurdity of teaching in the final stanza of his poem "Schoolsville," an imaginative sketch of a small town populated entirely by former students:

> Once in a while a student knocks on the door
> With a term paper fifteen years late
> Or a question about Yeats or double-spacing.
> And sometimes one will appear in a windowpane
> To watch me lecturing the wallpaper,
> quizzing the chandelier, reprimanding the air. (1988, 8)

The teacher who yearns to discuss the significance of Yeats's vision of the "Second Coming" is likely to discover that the question of double-spacing is—for this student at this time—a matter of much greater salience than is the rough beast that slouches toward Bethlehem. The teacher cannot say what matters most (and the reverent teacher does not try to) because that is always for the student to say. But the teacher whose sense of humor has not been irrevocably impaired may find amusement in the unpredictability of classroom life with its repeated reminder that the teacher is not, after all, the center of student learning. The poem points to another irony: the teacher cannot stop teaching. Even when the students are absent (literally or figuratively), the teacher is still "lecturing the wallpaper, / quizzing the chandelier, / reprimanding the air."

Galway Kinnell makes the same observation in his poem "The Schoolhouse" when he describes the teacher as "a man of letters" whose students are tramps: "A man of letters once asked the local tramps/to tea. No one came, and he read from Otway/and Chatterton to the walls" (Kinnell 1974, 83).

We may, when we are the one quizzing the chandelier and reading to the walls, see this as tragedy, the inevitable end of a life spent casting pearls before swine. But the reverent teacher laughs, knowing that the students are not swine and that if they have not been enthralled, it is because she has no pearls. In my careful exposition of Kinnell's poem, I was (for at least some of the students, some of the time) "lecturing the wallpaper," and I needed a plain-speaking student to reveal my irreverence with a punch line of a question, "I get that, but what does *Hellas* mean?"

So, the laughter of the reverent teacher is in part the nervous laugh of self-awareness, an embarrassed recognition of one's own limitations. But it is also a laugh of playfulness. Recall Ms. Hamilton who asks Richard, "Are you visiting or helping?" hears him say, "Helping," and continues without missing a beat, "Could you do it in a quieter voice?" We can, if we listen carefully, hear a hint of laughter in her words.

Love

When I showed *Random Harvest* to students in a class about the moral dimensions of schooling, they pretty much agreed that no one would behave as the Greer Garson character does in that movie. No real woman would seek out and discover her lost, amnesiac husband and then not tell him who she was. No real woman would wait to let him—if he could—remember on his own. No real woman would work as his secretary (without a word that she had once been his much-loved wife) and then agree to a sexless marriage of convenience. This is not, my students said, how real people act.

I suppose that my students are right, but I believe that even if this character's behavior cannot be a model for wives of amnesiac husbands, her story is nevertheless an instructive parable for the way in which the reverent teacher loves her students. The movie teaches that reverence asks us to surrender to love and to be illuminated by it.

But before I explore this claim, I have to ask if it's proper to talk about teachers loving students. After all, we don't want our teachers feeling (and certainly not expressing) romantic or erotic love for their students. Motherly love might be all right for teachers of young children, but we prefer our teachers to feel equal, cool emotion toward each of their students, and certainly nothing even as tamely romantic as that faithful love portrayed in *Random Harvest*. We are uncomfortable with the thought of *eros* in the classroom.

My response to this understandable uneasiness is that I think that Martha Nussbaum is right when she eloquently argues in *Upheavals of Thought* that love (the eros of Plato's *Symposium*) "is the basic form...of all human desire and motivation" (2001, 575). And this link between love and desire is the key to understanding "love's fundamental role in the entire ethical life" (ibid., 710). Without loving particular others, we cannot learn that "love...is not narrowly partial, but all-embracing in its concern, moved by compassion for all of fallen humanity. All people are really equal in its sight, and all are really people" (ibid., 577). It is through eros that we are led to "the illumination of love" (ibid., 671) that shines on all alike.

To gain access to this illumination, the reverent teacher must be open to "love's strange combination of agency with passivity." She must "see persons as centers of choice and freedom, but also as needy and demanding of care, as both independent and dependent" (Nussbaum 2001, 580). And it is here, with "love's strange combination of agency with passivity" that I return to *Random Harvest* and the sometime wife (known first in the movie as Paula—her stage name—and then as Margaret) who does not tell her amnesiac husband who she is.

Paula/Margaret could tell her husband Charles that she had loved him and married him when he was "Smithy," a soldier who lost his memory during World War I. She could tell him that she had borne him a son (now dead). But she knows that nothing she tells him can turn him into Smithy again. If he is going to love her, the emotions must come from within him. She can love him and give him every chance to remember and in this sense demonstrate agency, but she must also be passive, because what love desires is for him too, despite his neediness, to be independent.

The reverent teacher loves in this way. She knows that she can tell her students about the significance of the subjects she espouses. She can tell them about the elegant perfection of a mathematical proof or about the profound insight of a Shakespearean soliloquy or about the intricate interaction of the parts of a flower, but she also knows that her delight and enthusiasm and grasp are not signs of the students' engagement with the subject matter. Think again of Ms. Hamilton and her attempt to teach Richard how one behaves in a first-grade classroom. She could say, "Don't talk unless you're talking about your work, Richard." She could tell him to move his chair. She could take him aside and talk to him about the importance of letting others do their work. She could tell him that he'll need to be "responsible" when he gets to second grade. And all of this would address Richard's neediness, and none of it would encourage his independence.

But when Ms. Hamilton allows Richard to tell her (and the rest of the class) he's "helping," she treats him as an agent of "choice and freedom," and in this surrender, she illuminates his independence. This is how the reverent teacher loves.

Correct

When a reverent teacher believes that a student is moving away from the greater possibility, she must correct—despite the openness of her love and the humility arising from awareness of her limitations. Ms. Hamilton cannot ignore Richard's chatter. Correcting expresses the demand of reverence for the integrity of self-commitment. It is a severe demand, so I have chosen a severe verb (evoking, I suspect, an image of the nineteenth-century schoolmaster wielding the rod). The reverent teacher is not a cheerleader or a bystander to a student's learning or a mere facilitator of student projects. She takes a personal stand on the worthiness of student work.

The popular image of the teacher as a nonjudgmental facilitator is often traced back to things John Dewey wrote, such as the following passage from *School and Society* about the teacher making a "suggestion" for a student:

> A sympathetic teacher is quite likely to know more clearly than the child himself what his own instincts are and mean. But the suggestion must fit in with the dominant mode of growth in the child; it must serve simply as stimulus to bring forth more adequately what the child is already blindly striving to do. (1976, 89–90)

Seen as a recommendation to help a child do what the child wants to do, this passage readily suggests the image of teacher as mere facilitator, if not cheerleader. But it's important to keep in mind that Dewey is saying that the child does not know what she wants to do: she is "*blindly* striving." When Dewey says that the teacher knows better than the child what the child seeks, he has in mind the role of the curriculum. The teacher knows the greater possibilities of the child's impulses (to express, to communicate, to grasp) because the teacher knows humanity's achievements (from sculpture, philosophy, and plumbing to baking, electronics, and medicine). With this knowledge of the curriculum, the teacher sees what the child cannot—the greater possibility—something unlikely to be achieved through blind striving. That is, there will be times when the child's striving is mistaken, and the teacher must correct it. One of Dewey's examples (in *School and Society*) is of the child whose drawing of a tree and cave is not an accurate rendering:

> The cave is neatly set up on the hillside in an impossible way. You see the conventional tree of childhood—a vertical line with horizontal branches on each side. If the child had been allowed to go on repeating this sort of thing day by day, he would be indulging his instinct rather than exercising it. (1976, 28)

But the child was not allowed to indulge. Instead, he "was now asked to look closely at trees" (ibid., 28), to reevaluate his picture, and to revise. He was corrected. And his new picture (Dewey includes both pictures in *School and Society*) portrays trees that Dewey says are "possible ones, not mere symbols" (ibid., 29).

Now, I happen to agree with Dewey that the second picture has far more "poetic feeling" than the first picture does, and it even seems to me that the correcting of the student was done with love. The boy, says Dewey, "made again a free illustration, expressing his own imaginative thought, but controlled by detailed study of actual trees" (ibid., 29). It sounds as if the boy was allowed to act as an agent of "choice and freedom." He was not told that his first picture was wrong; he was instructed to only evaluate whether or not he was satisfied with it, and to use his own observations as the basis for this evaluation.

But I am not entirely confident about my reading of the events because it depends on unexamined assumptions about what counts as the curriculum against which the child's work was judged. Who says, for instance, that the trees in the picture ought to be "possible ones, not mere symbols"? Who says that pictures of a tree and cave need revision if they are not realistic or if they are conventional?

In our accountability-through-assessment world, many seek to avoid these questions by reducing learning to the acquisition of facts and the mastery of rubric-defined skills. Rubric in hand, our assessment of a picture of a tree and cave is supposed to become impersonal and exact. We tell ourselves that we are not advocating private values or a cultural stance: the picture needs revision because the score is too low, not because we personally find the picture shallow, careless, or conventional.

But I find no solace in this sleight-of-hand. When I interact with a student in a way that the student perceives as correction, I am not the impersonal, passive conduit of received truth; I am the active interpreter of a tradition. I am not a messenger delivering an assessment from Olympus or the experts in the field or the state board of education; *I* assess; *I* judge; *I* correct. Reverence demands the integrity of self-commitment.

At times, the judgment embodied in our correction (which is often a grade, rather than a formative suggestion) seems as inevitable as inserting a period at the end of this sentence. In one of my philosophy of education classes, two students turned in poems as their response to reading Dewey's *Democracy and Education*. One was a monologue in which Dewey spoke to George W. Bush about "democratic consensus." At my urging, the student later sent the poem to *Insights*, a newsletter of the John Dewey Society, and the poem was published (Sanders 2005). The other student turned in an acrostic poem spelling "John Dewey." The nine short lines lacked coherence and "poetic feeling," and five of them made inaccurate claims. The first student received an *A* for the assignment, the second an *F*.

While I am confident that I would assign the same grades again should the situation arise, I cannot say (as many teachers do) that "I did not give the grades—they were earned." I cannot remove myself from responsibility as the one who corrects and who sometimes determines that a student has failed. It is a terrible duty, and if it has not been done reverently—if it is not the voice of self-commitment—it is my failure too.

The Greater Possibility

When we talk about the quality of life, we typically talk about health and wealth and the satisfaction of bodily desires. Judging by television advertising in the early twenty-first century, a good life means low cholesterol, a high-limit credit card, and a pill for erectile dysfunction. It is a small advance on the good life described for me by some of my high school students in the 1970s—a sports car with personalized license plates, a big house, and a swimming pool filled with beer.

We recognize these as caricatures of the life we desire. We know that something is missing. But what is it?

Nearly the same question is posed in one of the scenes in *Random Harvest*. Watching the movie, we have seen Paula/Margaret become the wife of Charles Rainier, an industrial magnate and member of parliament. She wears designer gowns and sits in a private box at the symphony, where she is envied by all who see her. She lives in a mansion where she presides over a gala ball in honor of the prime minister. After the ball, Charles presents her with a fabulous necklace, and then, seeing the look on her face, he poses the question: "Is it enough?"

What an absurd question! How could beauty, wealth, power, and privilege not be enough? But within the world of the movie, we know it is not enough because we know it is not her greater possibility. Beauty, wealth, power, and privilege cannot be piled high enough to make happiness.

And in schools today, despite the incessant rhetoric, we know that higher test scores and higher graduation rates and more flattering international comparisons are not enough. The numbers do not matter if our children do not live meaningful lives. Our schools will never be genuinely successful if they do not help our children find their own greater possibility. We should ask our teachers not to fine tune and amplify their batteries of assessments but to listen, think, laugh, love, and correct. If we wish to nourish our children's greater possibility, we will teach them reverence by teaching them reverently.

References

Arendt, H. 1971. *Thinking/The Life of the Mind*. San Diego: Harcourt Brace.
Boostrom, R. 2005. *Thinking: The Foundation of Critical and Creative Learning in the Classroom*. New York: Teachers College Press.
Collins, B. 1988. Schoolsville. In *The Apple that Astonished Paris*, 7–8. Fayetteville and London: University of Arkansas Press.
Dewey, J. 1976. *The Middle Works, Volume 1: 1899–1901*. Edited by Jo Ann Boydston. Carbondale: Southern Illinois University Press.
———. 1980. *The Middle Works, Volume 9: 1916*. Edited by Jo Ann Boydston. Carbondale: Southern Illinois University Press.
Emerson, R. W. 1929. *The Complete Writings of Ralph Waldo Emerson*. New York: William H. Wise.
Jackson, P. W., R. E. Boostrom, and D. T. Hansen. 1993. *The Moral Life of Schools*. San Francisco: Jossey-Bass.
Kinnell, G. 1974. The Schoolhouse. In *The Avenue Bearing the Initial of Christ into the New World*, 83–85. Boston: Houghton Mifflin.
Miller, E., and J. Almon. 2009. *Crisis in the Kindergarten: Why Children Need to Play in School*. College Park, MD: Alliance for Childhood.
Mithen, S. 2006. *The Singing Neanderthals: The Origins of Music, Language, Mind and Body*. Cambridge, MA: Harvard University Press.

National Writing Project. 2009. "Billy Collins: A 'reader's poet' reads at NWP's 2009 annual meeting." Accessed March 27, 2010, http://www.nwp.org/cs/public/print/resource/3009.

Nussbaum, M. 2001. *Upheavals of Thought: The Intelligence of Emotion.* Cambridge: Cambridge University Press.

Plato. 1997. *Complete Works.* Edited by J. M. Cooper. Indianapolis, IN: Hackett.

Sacks, O. 2008. *Musicophilia: Tales of Music and the Brain.* New York: Vintage Books.

Sanders, B. A. 2005. John Dewey, in the wake of the 2004 election, speaks to George W. Bush on the nature of democratic consensus. *Insights* 37 (3): 3–5.

2

Reverence and Love in Teaching

Daniel P. Liston

Introduction

A few years ago I was seated around a seminar table that included Bob Moses, Eleanor Duckworth, Linda Mizell, Bill Ayers, Lorrie Shepard, Lisa Delpit, Dr. Vincent Harding, Mike Apple, George Stranahan, and a few others. We were gathered that day to honor Bob Moses's accomplishments with the Algebra Project. The early part of the day was devoted to a seminar focused on the history and future of progressive education. In the afternoon Bob Moses delivered a talk to the University of Colorado community on quality education as a civil right. A number of questions were posed and addressed throughout the seminar, including What do we mean by, and what should "progressive education" look like in this century's upcoming decades? During the ensuing discussion the topic turned to teachers' capacities to educate all children and Mike Apple argued that knowing a student or colleague "really" was not a feat we humans could expect to achieve. In teaching other people's children we are severely limited in our knowledge and understanding of others' motives, interests, and capacities. In teaching all children we are constrained. Stepping into someone else's shoes, so as to guide them educationally, was neither a feasible nor an advisable instructional move. When I heard Apple, my major professor, claim that our knowledge of others especially our students was severely restricted, I had to pause. One of my core beliefs has been that teaching and learning benefit from a kind of reverential classroom ethos, one in which an attentive love is practiced and knowledge of others is gained.

We are limited in our capacity to understand students or others. But such limitations need not cordon off attempts to see our students, their parents, and our colleagues more clearly. Recognition of this limitation need not move teachers away from attempts at understanding others, but rather toward a predisposition, a stance or virtue, that some have called "reverence." Paul Woodruff (2001) maintains that reverence "begins in a deep understanding of human limitations; from this grows the capacity to be in awe of whatever we believe lies outside our control...The capacity for awe, as it grows, brings with it the capacity for respecting fellow human beings, flaws and all" (3). Woodruff argues that "reverence is the capacity for a range of feelings and emotions that are linked; it is a sense that there is something larger than a human being, accompanied by capacities for awe, respect and shame" (ibid., 63).

In this chapter I will argue that embracing these limitations entails not only the virtue of reverence but also the virtue and practice of attentive love. Reverence entails a respectful understanding of our limitations and calls forth both awe and respect toward others. When we fail we feel shame. But in our educational settings (and perhaps in other settings) it is difficult to conceive how reverence without attentive love can call forth awe or respect. To be in awe of and have respect for students requires that we attempt to see the mystery that our students truly are. The practice of attentive love enables teachers to see their students a bit more clearly. Attentive love entails the following: the presumption that good exists within each student; the attempt to discern and see our students more clearly and justly; and the understanding that in order to see more clearly we need to reduce the noise of our selves. Attentive love in teaching is frequently a struggle and a sacrifice. It is a struggle and a sacrifice to see beyond our egoistic selves so as to see our students more clearly. Utilizing the work of Paul Woodruff, Simone Weil, Iris Murdoch, Sara Ruddick, and Mark Edmundson I argue that, and explore the ways in which, reverence and attentive love are components of a worthwhile teaching stance.

Reverence

Talk of reverence in the classroom makes me look into the history of my past schooling. It also recalls the "enforced reverence" of my Catholic educational background. In the presence of Catholic Dominican nuns, from grades three through six, we proceeded to mass for weekly celebrations. When kneeling in the pews our bottoms could not rest on the benches behind us, our hands had to be clasped in prayer-like fashion, and we could not whisper to our similarly embodied neighbor. We were advised to kneel properly and refrain from neighborly conversations so as to show the proper awe and respect while in God's house. Ceremony abounded in this Midwestern Catholic upbringing and it was ceremony oriented toward a reverential respect for God and the church. I learned Latin, served as an altar boy for mass and other church rituals, and understood the authority of my religious educators. But I can't say that I experienced a sense of transcendent awe and wonder. All too often I felt an awareness of human power and authority but not a sense of awe and wonder.

Instead I came to an educational appreciation of reverence, awe, and wonder, when my secular teachers enabled me to join in their search for truth and beauty. It was in high school that this occurred—Burris High School, then the laboratory school of Ball State Teachers College. The teachers who taught me the most loved their subjects and, in their own fashion, cared for their students.[1] Dr. Keener, my demanding high school social studies teacher, showed us how history illuminated our worlds. He made us sit up straight in class and take copious notes; and we understood these demands as marks of his respect for us. Mr. Fleenor, my geometry teacher, lured us into the world of geometry by helping us to think logically, clearly, and elegantly. When we entered his room we knew we would work at it together. Miss Dutro, my biology teacher, could look at a roadside weed and show us its ecological niche. She turned weeds into fascinating subjects and she also believed we were fascinating. All three of these teachers taught with an individually crafted sense of reverence, a love of learning, and attention to the students they taught. Their invitation to learn amounted to more than classroom order and an offering of facts, skills, and concepts to master. It included all of that, and much, much more. It was based on their love of learning and desire to connect student with their beloved subject matter. These were master teachers in whose classrooms I felt reverence, awe, and wonder.

How did they do it? How did these teachers bring to the classroom that sense of reverence, awe, and wonder? Paul Woodruff is helpful here. Focusing on teaching,[2] Woodruff underscores three central elements of reverential teaching: the teacher's devotion to inquiry and a search for truth; a recognition that together, teacher and students are trying to understand something important; and the teacher's ability to see the sometimes hidden drives and desires of their students. Woodruff writes that "What lies behind the teacher's respect (for students) is devotion to the truth" (2001, 203). And it is this devotion to the truths contained in each teacher's "enormous subject" that animates and motivates some teachers' work. But in the classroom the teacher does not embark on this journey with an enormous subject alone—they are accompanied by others. Woodruff writes that "Reverence in the classroom calls for a sense of awe in the face of the truth and a recognition by teachers and students of their places in the order of learning" (ibid., 191). Later he adds that "teachers and students will respect each other insofar as they recognize that they belong together in a common effort—trying to understand something that is important to understand" (ibid., 202). But teachers frequently do not adequately convey the magnitude of their subject and often students are not initially motivated to pursue the subject at hand. Woodruff writes:

> As a teacher, you will not be able to respect students if you cannot find that they want to learn anything, but people are curious by nature, and the more you bring students' natural curiosity to light, the better you will be able to respect them. Part of good teaching is the ability to discover good things about people who seem to be bad students (ibid.,190).

Phrasing the obstacle to successful learning in this manner sounds a bit odd. Trying to discover "good things about people who seem to be bad students" may be a central task in some educational situations. But more often it seems to be the case that, as teachers, we are attempting to discern those features of our students that link to and engage their motivation to learn the subject at hand, a subject we love. We attempt to discover good things about students so as to link them to the assigned and valued topics. If we attempt to spoon-feed, deliver-under-threat, or demand students' attention – we run the risk of misdirecting and miseducating.

And so how do we find out the "good things" about our students? How do we uncover and give life to the natural curiosity that lies within? We need to start from a stance of "attentive love." For it is through attending lovingly to others that we come to a better understanding of who our students are and how our subject might connect with their aspirations and dreams.

Attentive Love[3]

In the last century at least three philosophers developed and articulated conceptual elements of attentive love: Simone Weil, Iris Murdoch, and Sara Ruddick. In various writings Weil elaborates the qualities of "attention" and the role it plays in developing a spiritually and deistically oriented attentive love (Weil 1951; 1963; 1981; 1998). For Weil, attentive love serves as a sort of antidote to the force, power, and gravity that pervade our material lives (Springsted 1986). Based upon Weil's elaboration, Murdoch and Ruddick articulate their conceptions. In Murdoch's first substantial philosophical text, *The Sovereignty of Good*, she transforms Weil's deistic understandings of attentiveness into a nondeistic but nevertheless spiritual view of love, beauty, and the Good (Murdoch 1971). Sara Ruddick, a philosopher and a mother, explores the commingling of reason and emotion in one of life's most precious and difficult endeavors, that of being a parent. In *Maternal Thinking*, she takes Weil's and Murdoch's spiritually aligned conceptions of attentive love and elaborates a more secular view (Ruddick 1989, 119–123).

All three writers contrast the positive qualities of attentive love with conditions or orientations that diminish it. For all three, attentive love is an antidote to a prevalent force in our world; and I'd like to claim reverence and attentive love as antidotes to the dominant forces in our public school classrooms. The classroom of the twenty-first century does not seem to be a place where reverence and attentive love are encouraged. Highly prescribed and enforced learning seem to characterize these educational settings. Legislatively prescribed and bureaucratically enforced standards predominate. Neither reverence nor love typify our teachers' and students' classroom lives. Since we live in enforced learning settings, not reverential contexts, these settings of force need to be understood.

Among these three women philosophers, Simone Weil elaborates and typifies this concern for force best. In her essay "The *Iliad*, or Poem of Force," Weil portrays a view of human interactions in which power and force prevail (1981). In war, Weil observes, both victim and victor believe that the exercise of force is the only option and *the* heroic route. She believes both to be deluded. For Weil, the *Iliad's* central character is not the warrior but force itself. In the *Iliad*, as in life, force seduces, diminishes, destroys, and prevails; and war represents the extreme, not the exception, in human interactions. Concerning Weil's *Iliad* commentary, Eric Springsted writes:

> The relations between the inner person and force are not essentially different in other spheres of life. Because we fear death and nothingness, we seek to gain more and more power to fend off the threat. Then two things happen to us. First, because we can never truly be possessors of force, we become possessed by it, and because one force tends to increase indefinitely until checked by another, we rarely exercise any self-limitation in the struggle for power.... The race for power... [is present]... as we seek to increase our wealth, security, and prestige. The second consequence of our blind quest for prestige, then, is our coming to identify true human life with what is ultimately only an exercise of power. At this point we begin to see ourselves as essentially the sum of what we possess and wield, and our longing for anything beyond what we can gain by force starts to degenerate. (1986, 23–24)

For Weil, the only way to escape the predicament of force is through the gift of grace. "It is only by the gift of one beyond the play of forces that we can ever escape the illusions of force" (Springsted 1986, 24). This gift of grace is present in reverential educational settings and attained, in part, through recognizing the enormous power of the subject at hand and attentive love. Through attentive love we can more capably create the conditions for connecting students to the natural curiosity that lies within. Through attentive love we create the basis for respecting the student's search for truth and understanding.

Elements of Attentive Love

In the reverential teacher's attempt to connect student and world, attentive love entails the following: the presumption that good exists within each student; the attempt to discern and see our students more clearly and justly; and the understanding that in order to see more clearly we need to reduce the noise of our selves. Attentive love in teaching is frequently a struggle and a sacrifice. It is a struggle and a sacrifice to see beyond our egoistic selves so as to see our students more clearly.

The Good Within and Beyond

It is not unusual for teachers to overlook the actual and potential "good" that exists within each student. When teaching is construed (for us or by us) as controlling and directing others, discerning this good is not a priority or a need. When teaching is defined solely as drilling and skilling kids to achieve higher standardized test scores, we do not honor and respect students. But when teaching is viewed as a way to help others take part in the challenges and pleasures of understanding our political, cultural, and natural worlds and become more capable in participating in and transforming these worlds, then we frequently need to affirm and understand (as much as we can) our students' goodness.

It is an act of faith and a persistently reinforced belief that we seek to understand, to reach out beyond ourselves for "that which is good." It is a desire that may not always be consciously present and certainly conflicts with other desires and needs. But it is a yearning that defines, in part, what it means to be human. It is a desire that Simone Weil captures quite well. She writes:

> At the center of the human heart, is the longing for an absolute good, a longing which is always there and never [adequately] appeased by any object in this world. (quoted in Bell 1998, 79)

A yearning for transcendence, a longing for something greater than ourselves is what Weil uncovers. We long to reach beyond ourselves, to see and participate in something larger than ourselves. In educational settings it is the "enormous subject," the immensity of the topic at hand that can serve as that realm beyond ourselves, the something larger.

Another element in our students' (and our own) goodness is the expectation that, in this world, they will be treated decently. Weil writes:

> At the bottom of the heart of every human being, from earliest infancy until the tomb, there is something that goes on indomitably expecting, in the teeth of all experience of crimes committed, suffered, and witnessed, that good and not evil will be done to him. It is this above all that is sacred in every human being. (quoted in Bell 1998, 79)

Weil maintains that each and every human being is sacred. Our students are sacred because of these yearnings: they expect and search for good in this world and yearn for a good beyond. When we approach students with this understanding we respect and honor them. We honor their good within and we respect their search for the good.

When teaching we connect students with material that has, among other purposes, the potential to take them beyond themselves, to attend to the world and themselves more clearly, and to act in ways that are decent and loving. In teaching, we can attend lovingly to the good in our students so that they, in turn, can develop their search for the good. Teaching and learning, with its intellectual and emotional interrogation of the world—when pursued with depth, vigor, and pleasure—can engage and refine students' attentive qualities. And in order to enable this engagement, teachers need to assume, honor, and pursue the good that lies within each student. It becomes, as Woodruff underscores, a basis for the respect that is part and parcel of the awe, wonder, and respect we can develop toward others and ourselves.

Discerning Students Clearly and Justly

Sara Ruddick writes in her book *Maternal Thinking* that attentive love "implies and rewards a faith that...to the loving eye the lovable will be revealed.... Attentive love, or loving attention, represents a kind of knowing that takes truthfulness as its aim but makes truth serve lovingly the person known" (1989, 119–120). In teaching, this requires that we look with loving, clear-sighted attention to our students to connect them with the educational tasks at hand. Attentive love in teaching readies students for an engagement with the worlds around them through the curriculum.

In elementary settings when students are young and skills undeveloped, in high school when students have become numb to learning, or at most any educational level when beginning a new topic of study, we, as teachers, need to prepare students for the tasks, challenges, and pleasures of learning. Attentive love enables teachers to see the student more clearly and identify what preparation and/or further connections should occur.

So what are the qualities of this attentiveness? Iris Murdoch claims that we attend throughout the moments of our days. We look at our students, observe their mannerisms, frustrations, interests, anxieties, dress, and fascinations. We hear their concerns. Murdoch writes: "In particular situations 'reality' as that which is revealed to the patient eye of love is an idea entirely comprehensible to the ordinary person. The task of attention goes on all the time and at apparently empty and everyday moments we are 'looking,' making those little peering efforts of imagination which have such important cumulative results" (1971, 40; 43). Teachers observe and note students' characteristics and features; they do this daily, throughout the week, and during the semester. Attentive teachers can speak volumes about their students. In order to see and speak those volumes, these teachers have to suspend temporarily their own expectations, bracket their agendas, and set aside their concerns so as to apprehend the student's reality on his or her own terms. This is not an easy task; it requires effort, discipline, and sacrifice.

Murdoch reminds us that when we attempt to attend lovingly to others, it can be a complicated endeavor:

> Human beings are far more complicated and enigmatic and ambiguous than languages or mathematical concepts, and selfishness operates in a much more devious and frenzied manner in our relations with them.... Our attachments tend to be selfish and strong, and the transformation of our loves from selfishness to unselfishness is sometimes hard even to conceive of.... The love which brings the right answer is an exercise of justice and realism and really looking. The difficulty is to keep the attention fixed upon the real situation and to prevent it from returning surreptitiously to the self with consolations of self-pity, resentment, fantasy, and despair.... It is a task to come to see the world as it is. (1971, 91)

When engaged in intellectual and pedagogical pursuits, our selfish desires can obstruct our understandings. We can impose our meanings on historical reconstructions or, because of our frustrations of the moment, fail to grasp a mathematical algorithm. Our egos can get in the way. In our pedagogical interactions, we may be much more prone to see obscurely. It is difficult to see our students unencumbered by the noise of our teacher egos. Our own conceptions, anxieties, satisfactions, and dreams can get in the way. There is in teachers, as humans, the inclination to see the world as we want to see it, not to view it with loving kindness. It is a struggle to see others and the world with loving, clear-sighted attention. It is an effort to reduce the noise of our egoistic selves.

Reducing the Noise of the Self

It is a struggle to attend to students. The struggle is not that attentive love requires attending to each and every student in all of our class sessions. Rather it is a task to suspend our own expectations, bracket our own agendas, and set aside our concerns so as to see the matter at hand from our students' point of view. The degree of difficulty varies. With some students, we are able to see fairly clearly the obstacles and issues at hand, and we can facilitate their learning. With others, it may take a few days of trying on different interpretations, distinct framings, so as to see the student before us with clear sighted attention. And yet with others, we have to examine not only their situation but ourselves; we have to look at what in us is getting in the way of seeing them more clearly. Lisa Delpit, the accomplished literacy scholar, writes about this quality of attention as a form of listening, as a way of attending to others when differences become obstacles. She writes that when this occurs we need

> a very special kind of listening, listening that requires not only open eyes and ears, but open hearts and minds. We do not really see through our eyes or hear through our ears, but through our beliefs. To put our beliefs on hold is to cease to exist as ourselves for a moment—and that is not easy. It is painful as well, because it means turning yourself inside out, giving up your own sense of who you are, and being willing to see yourself in the unflattering light of another's angry gaze. It is not easy, but it is the only way to learn what it might feel like to be someone else and the only way to start the dialogue. (1988, 297)

How do we put our beliefs on hold to attend to the other before us? How do we reduce the noise of our egos? Sara Ruddick and Iris Murdoch lay out some rudimentary features: we talk with others; we attempt to see the good in the situation or student; and we refocus our attention on an object that is a source of contemplation and energy.

There are times when in order to see the student or situation more clearly we have to refocus our gaze, look away in an effort to gain some distance and detachment from the current scene. Murdoch talks of prayer and reorientation as two options. Not all of us are spiritually oriented. However, we have within us the power to redirect our gaze on something of value. In this vein, Murdoch writes: "Whatsoever things are true, whatsoever things are honest, whatsoever things are just, whatsoever things are pure, whatsoever things are lovely, whatsoever things of good report; if there be any virtue, and if there be any praise, think on these things" (1971, 56). Conversations with others, refocusing on the good within the situation or student, and a reorientation of our gaze allows us a degree of detachment from the noise of ourselves. None is, for sure, a guaranteed method. But all seem to provide a measure of redirection and detachment.

Attentive Love and Reverence

If we value an education that is oriented, in part, to awe and wonder and undergirded with an attitude of respect, then it would seem that reverence and attentive love would be part of that effort. Reverence, as Woodruff states, begins as a recognition of our human limitations and results in the capacity for awe of what lies outside our control. Reverence, it seems, is a very human and humanizing virtue. Here I have claimed that this capacity for respecting and honoring others, especially students in the classroom, is facilitated through the virtue of attentive love. Reverence and attentive love seem to serve each other well. With reverence we recognize the inherent limitations in our efforts to know and understand, as well as to live in this world. And with attentive love we attempt to see others, ourselves, and our worlds more clearly. We are limited and restricted but we are not without powerful inner resources. The resources of attentive love do not enable us to transcend our human limitations. But this process—through which we attempt to affirm the good in our students, see them more clearly—and reduce the noise of our teaching and personal selves, is a practice that enables teachers to connect the student to the subject at hand powerfully and reverentially.

One way to further illustrate and explore this commingling of reverence and attentive love is to interrogate a living example. Mark Edmundson offers one in his memoir, *Teacher: The One Who Made the Difference*. Frank Lears was the teacher who walked into Medford High School in Massachusetts, Edmundson's working-class high school, during his senior year, and seemingly transformed his life. As a result of Lears' philosophy class, his persistent questioning, curricular experimentation, and attentive listening, Edmundson began a lifelong task of self-understanding through literary and textual explorations. It seems to me that both reverence and attentive love were factors in Edmundson's educational transformation.

Frank Lears arrived at Medford High in the early 1970s and stayed for one year. Having graduated from Harvard, Lears taught a group of high school seniors an introductory philosophy class. Initially offering a curriculum based on an oral, classroom reading of Will and Ariel Durant's introductory philosophy textbook, Lears sat his students in a seminar circle and peppered them with questions. Slowly, very slowly, the class took on a life of its own. Edmundson writes that Lears' instruction

> wasn't about himself and his ideas per se. He didn't...want you to think the way he did...(instead) He wanted you simply to be able to ask yourself the kinds of questions about what you believed, and why, that he himself might ask. He was like a mirror who gave you back to yourself.... And he spared no one...his hard-edged questions. (2002, 215)

Edmundson relates that in one particular class session Lears pursued the topic of solitude asking "What does it mean to be alone? Is it possible? What would it mean to be genuinely by oneself?" (ibid., 216–217). Lears called on Nora, who Edmundson describes as one of the high school's princesses, a member of the elect who were destined for happiness. In response to Lears' questions Nora elaborated, honestly and directly, and at length

> a litany of defenses against being alone. She mentioned listening to the radio and talking on the phone, then playing songs and the conversations over in her mind. She cited a span of other strategies, ending, perceptively enough, with expectation, our habit of blocking out the present by waiting for things to happen in the future. "Waiting," she said. "Waiting for things to happen to you is a way of not being alone."
> "And why," asked Lears, "is it hard to be alone?"
> "Because," Nora answered, "I might start to think about things. I might start to think about my life." (Ibid., 217)

Edmundson relates that Nora—the embodiment of high school beauty, intelligence, and perfection—had just admitted that all was not right in her world. It was shocking. She had been honest and unapologetic about her condition. Edmundson observes that "If she could do such a thing—talk candidly, self-critically, without pretense—perhaps the rest of us could too" (ibid., 218).

It's not clear how many of the other students joined Nora's forthright, in-class engagement and pursuit. However, it is clear from Edmundson's account that others, besides Nora and himself, were transformed by Lears' instruction. For it seems that Lears devoted himself to engaging others in inquiry—in a search for truth. In Lears' class that search was enormous and extensive as well as immediate and intense—a critical examination of life and self. This reverential devotion to inquiry, to a search for truths and worldly understanding was something that Lears practiced and wanted to share with his students. Edmundson writes: "What Lears really wanted, I believe, was simply for people to think. He wanted them to examine their old ways of doing things, and if the result of the examination was that they liked those ways well enough or that they wanted to get more conservative, more...that was all right. So long as they took up a distanced position from their beliefs and had a look" (ibid., 194).

Lears accomplished this reverential inquiry, in part, through listening, through attending to his students. Edmundson recalls that

> I can still remember the way Lears settled his gaze on me as I talked. His soft brown eyes were mesmerizing; it was as if a deer had somehow acquired preternatural intelligence and could combine warmth with the greatest level of comprehension. It struck me then for the first time that when this guy listened to you, the experience was of a different order from when anyone else did. He wasn't thinking about anything else. He was completely poised on your thoughts.... when Lears listened...it felt as though you were being fed something very good and sustaining. And when he stopped listening because your turn was up, it was as though earthly ambrosia was being taken from you....
>
> And the harder and more humanely he listened, the more anxious we felt. The fact that he seemed ready to credit our inane reactions, to respond to them as though they were long-pondered elements of contoured philosophic systems, started out by making us feel better, more comfortable and self-assured. But the listening intensity also somehow threw the issue back onto us. Is this really what we believe? Is it what we think? (Ibid. 119–120)

We have in Frank Lears (as memorialized by Edmundson) a case of reverence in teaching, seemingly informed and facilitated by attentive love. Lears' instruction appears to have been motivated by a devotion to inquiry, a search for truth—on his own and with his students. In order to engage and invite others along he attended lovingly to his students. He looked for the good in each and assumed some good in the world at large; attempted to see his students and enable them to see themselves more clearly; and must have quieted some of his own internal noise in the process.

In the course of the year at Medford High, Lears changed the philosophy curriculum—from an overview of the central philosophical questions (via Will and Ariel Durant) to a thematic exploration of the oppression of conformity (by way of Albert Camus' *The Stranger*, Ken Kesey's *One Flew Over the Cuckoo's Nest*, Sigmund Freud's *Group Psychology*, and Herman Hesse's *Siddartha*). He accomplished this in part (I believe) by diagnosing and attending to his students' high school existential condition. He seems to have believed that the theme of conformity and other closely related concerns would engage their search, their desire to learn. With Edmundson he was spot on. Through his searching questions and altered curricular format Lears changed the terms of education (in one classroom) at Medford High and transformed a few lives in the process. And what's more, Lears did so without embodying a number of the clichéd features the customary good-natured, warm-hearted, and transformative teacher. Edmundson ends his memoir by noting that Lears was a great teacher.

> …in large measure because, at least at the start, he clearly did not like us much at all…He did not love us as individuals or as a group. But I believe he did love freedom – he wanted to live among free people, in part because it made his own life richer…. [and] for all the minor miracle of what he accomplished with us, he was no missionary. He served us but also himself. (Ibid., 265–266)

In an era in which the obsessive and politically correct mantra is that quality education must focus broadly on student learning or narrowly on student achievement—it is refreshing to read an account of a reverent and loving teacher who was committed to his own as well as his students' search for truth and self-understanding. Talk of reverence and attentive love can lead many to a pious, clichéd image of good teaching. It need not be that way. These days it is engaging to read of an accomplished teacher who was neither saint nor hero, but rather a flawed human being living his loves, attending to others, learning and teaching.

Conclusion

Seeing the good within students, attempting to see them more clearly, and reducing the noise of the observing self are tasks that seem to arise with a reverential attitude toward learning. In searching for truth in the world it seems helpful to search for the truth in our students. In order to connect and convey our understandings of the world to our students it helps to have insights into both the world and students. The two efforts seem to go hand-in-hand.

Postscript: Thirty-two years ago I knocked on Mike Apple's office door wanting to know if he would accept another doctoral student, one who respected and valued his work but found parts of *Ideology and Curriculum* problematic. He said he would. During those five years of graduate work it became evident to me that he brought a strong sense of reverence to the study of schooling. He was engaged in a search for understanding our public schools and their multifaceted contexts. He entertained and engaged disagreements, countervailing views, and alternative understandings. It was clear that his inquiry was an invitation for us, his graduate students, to go further. As his students we pursued a greater understanding of schools and schooling and we believed we were involved in something quite important. Mike did this without much fanfare and more than a smidgeon of attentive love. Protests and statements to the contrary—he sought and saw our desire to learn as well as aspects of our character.

Notes

1. In "Despair and Love in Teaching" I comment on these teachers' capacities.
2. Woodruff focuses on the "silent" teacher. Here I will draw inferences from his elaboration of the "silent teacher" stance to other valuable and more voluble approaches.
3. In an earlier version of this chapter presented at the American Educational Research Association I outlined these critical aspects of attentive love as well as in a review essay entitled "Critical pedagogy and attentive love." *Studies in Philosophy and Education* 27 (5): 387–392.

References

Bell, R. H. 1998. *Simone Weil: The Way of Justice as Compassion.* New York: Rowman & Littlefield.
Delpit, L. 1988. The silenced dialogue: Power and pedagogy in education other people's children. *Harvard Educational Review* 58 (3): 280–298.
Edmundson, M. 2002. *Teacher: The One Who Made the Difference.* New York: Random House.
Liston, D. 2002. Despair and Love in Teaching. In *Stories of the Courage to Teach: Honoring the Teacher's Heart.* Edited by Sam M. Intrator, 42–53. San Francisco: Jossey-Bass.
———. 2008. Critical pedagogy and attentive love. *Studies in Philosophy and Education* 27 (5): 387–392.
Murdoch, I. 1971. *The Sovereignty of Good.* New York: Schocken.
Ruddick, S. 1989. *Maternal Thinking.* Boston: Beacon Press.

Springsted, E. 1986. *Simone Weil and the Suffering of Love*. Cambridge, MA: Cowley.

Weil, S. 1951. *Waiting for God*. New York: G. P. Putnam's Sons.

———. 1963. *Gravity and Grace*. London: Routledge and Kegan Paul.

———. 1981. *The Iliad or the Poem of Force*. Translated by Mary McCarthy. Wallingford, PA: Pendle Hill Pamphlet #91.

———. 1998. *Simone Weil*. Edited by Eric Springsted. Maryknoll, NY: Orbis Books.

Woodruff, P. 2001. *Reverence: Reviving a Forgotten Virtue*. New York: Oxford University Press.

3

"To Seek by Way of Silence"

Michael Dale

Introduction

Our students are busy, busy taking classes, busy working part-time (sometimes full-time) jobs, busy talking/texting on their cell phones, busy surfing the Internet searching for information to complete the most recently assigned paper or project. All of this busy-ness occurs within the contexts of environments filled with the visual and auditory noise of twenty-first-century American life inside and outside of classrooms and schools. The activities and the environment are the taken-for-granted milieu in the lives of our students. In our own lives as well if we are honest with ourselves. We do not, like Jakob in Anne Michael's novel *Fugitive Pieces* (1997), know how "to seek by way of silence" (111). It is important to point out that the silence I reveal in this chapter is of a particular kind, because as Paul Woodruff argues, "Excessive noise and [a particular species] of silence both fall away from the ideal of reverence in the classroom" (2001, 193).

It seems crucial to recognize that the buzz of modern life has both external and internal impact and makes all of us, especially our students, to simply accept the busy-ness and noisiness as an unalterable and essentially benign way of being in today's world. Paloma, the delightful twelve-year-old protagonist in Muriel Barberry's *The Elegance of the Hedgehog*, describes her "Profound Thought No. 5" on discovering that her sister, Colombe, works deliberately to deny Paloma the silence she desires:

> I think she [Colombe] discovered this by chance. It would never have crossed her mind spontaneously that somebody might actually need silence. That silence helps you to go inward, that anyone interested in something more than just life outside actually needs silence: this, I think,

is not something Colombe is capable of understanding, because her inner space is as chaotic and noisy as the street outside. (2008, 84–85)

If Paloma is correct (and I believe that she is) then the external and internal noisiness of life is not benign; it is in fact an obstacle in our lives. As Woodruff reminds us, "Reverent respect cannot grow just anywhere" (2001, 203). Susan Neiman in her book *Moral Clarity* argues that the Enlightenment's hostility to traditional religion was not a disregard for the value of reverence in our lives. In fact, she claims that "The Enlightenment denied piety to make room for reverence. If piety is a matter of fear and trembling, reverence is a matter of awe and wonder" (2009, 241). In this chapter I hope to show that the noisiness of our lives and classrooms, the omnipresent buzz of linear, instrumental, means-ends reasoning, is impoverished soil for the growth of reverence. By instrumental reasoning I mean a perspective of education that sees learning and teaching almost exclusively in terms of economic outcomes to be gained; a perspective in which knowledge and understanding become commodities, variables in an economic calculation and the relations between teachers and students acquire the sensibilities of a business transaction (Dale 2004). An unhealthy and distorting emphasis in teaching and learning on (economic) competitiveness creates a fear-filled environment; the wonder of mathematics or the natural world understood through biology is almost completely absent.

As I examine education, in particular teacher education in this chapter, I will have reason to question and qualify Paloma's "profound thought" that silence is solely a matter of turning inward. Silencing our internal noise is necessary in order to see and hear clearly the people with whom we engage and interact, and the world that we inhabit. Paloma actually points us in this direction; her sister only stumbles upon Paloma's need for silence: "And as for the frosting on the cake, for some obscure reason Colombe, who most of the time is totally insensitive to what's going on with other people, has figured out that what I dread more than anything else in life is noise" (Barberry 2008, 84). The reason I think is not really obscure; Colombe's "total insensitivity to what's going on with other people," her inability to see that her sister needed silence, is a consequence of an "inner space as chaotic and noisy as the street outside." Silence, as I describe it in this chapter, is necessary not only to "to inward" but to also see and receive what lies outside of us. Drawing upon both works of fiction and nonfiction that I read with my students in teacher education (e.g., Kathleen Hill's short story *The Anointed*, Annie Dillard's *Pilgrim at Tinker Creek,* and Margret Buchmann's *The Practicality of Contemplative Attention: Devoted Thought That Is Not Deluded*) this chapter begins to describe why it is important for prospective and practicing teachers to nurture and value silence in their lives and the lives of their students. This argument recognizes that silence and stillness are antithetical to the prevailing ethos of schools and schooling, including teacher education.

I begin here to show the truth of Shapiro's claim that "school, to a very great extent, is the very embodiment of the culture of production; doing, performing, showing is the very axis of school life. We so much need there opportunities that can cultivate the Sabbath consciousness of stillness, reflection, and appreciation for what is" (2006, 198). In doing so, the wonder and awe of a world outside of us, the wonder and awe of reverence can grow.

Noisy Schools and Classrooms

Our classrooms and schools are seen by most students (and teachers) as places for "getting": getting information or knowledge, getting the right answer, getting a degree, or for producing or achieving something. In addition, the time spent in learning settings, whether public K-12 schools or universities, is seen as something to be "gotten through" as quickly as possible. This ethos of "getting through" and getting done is consistent with and reinforces the prevailing instrumental orientation toward the world and others, a utilitarian value outlook where the ends of our thought and action are given and accepted without any question except how to "get" them. In fact, instrumental reason and a utilitarian value outlook are major elements of the din of modern life for our students and, as I will argue in this chapter, this internal and external noise is not a benign condition. It is within the context of this noise that students, including prospective and practicing teachers in our teacher education programs, come to frame and understand the purposes and meaning of learning and teaching. The knowledge-seeking learner sees the world and a cognitive understanding of that world as something to be controlled, mastered, and used. The visceral metaphor of regurgitating information on tests or in performing and producing what is required in classrooms and schools is simply the consequence of seeing the world and others as objects for ingestion or consumption.

It does not matter whether the "objects" are found in nature (e.g., trees, muskrats) or the works of human expression in the arts and sciences; the complexity of what lies outside of us is reduced to elements that we can manipulate, conquer, and master. The classroom mantra "What is the use of learning *this*?" is not only seen as a respectable question, it is considered the only question worth posing, the only question that could possibly reveal the value and worth of what is being taught and learned. The cliché about not taking the time to stop and smell the roses is not less true because it has become a shibboleth. A sensual pleasure perhaps, but a waste of time nonetheless. The scent of a flower isn't something you master; it is a gift you receive with gratitude. Here we begin to see the distinction that should be drawn between "getting" and "receiving."

The noise is pervasive in our lives and in our educational institutions. Our lives are busy and noisy and the response seems: So what? A first step in responding to this question must begin to articulate what is missing in our lives when our orientation is consistently a stance of asking what we can get from an encounter. We must begin to ask our students whether this instrumental stance toward learning and toward the world around them is impoverished and should start to highlight the ways in which the noise and instrumental value orientation of their lives may be construed as a limitation. Along with these questions we suggest that another path exists that could transform our consciousness and enable us to become more receptive and responsive to the reality of the world and others. One of the ways in which this can be done, we argue, is through the engagement with rich and compelling narrative and philosophical writings that illustrate and invite this transformation through the very rich and descriptive language of the readings. They are not textbooks designed for speed reading to highlight the useful information for a test. By learning "to seek by way of silence" our students are presented with and engaged in a noninstrumental way of being in the world; they are shown vivid and enlivening alternative, noninstrumental, nonutilitarian answers to the questions, "Why learn?" and "Why teach? In this chapter I will highlight several particular readings because they underscore this quieter way of being in the world both outside and inside a classroom.

Turning Inward and Gazing Outward

Reflection and Contemplation. I imagine many people use these two concepts interchangeably, at least in reference to human mental activity. Even the *Oxford English Dictionary* in defining the mental meaning for reflection uses contemplation as a synonym. This is certainly understandable, as reflection means a "bending back or turning" back of light off the surface of objects. This idea of "bending back" certainly seems to be connected to the commonplace understanding that reflective thought is a matter of turning inward for self-knowledge. Contemplation, on the other hand, has at its root meaning the act of turning outward, "to look at with continued attention, gaze upon, view, observe." I point out this slight, but significant, etymological difference to highlight that reverential silence is not so much an inward turning as it is a thoughtful beholding of what lies outside of us. We need such silence not so much in order to be able to hear ourselves think, but to provide for us the conditions under which we can see and hear what our eyes and ears are turned toward. In an important sense the "self" is silenced in order to hear the "other." I am reminded of the Nobel Laureate biologist Barbara McClintock who attributed her work in genetics to "listening to the corn."

> Paloma speaks of a silence that "helps you to go inward." While I don't wish to deny the silence required for this kind of reflective thought, I want to suggest that Paloma herself does not move away from her planned suicide on her thirteenth birthday until she listens to Madame Renée Michel's story (her sister Lisette had died tragically at a young age, scarring Madame Michel in the aftermath). It is then that Paloma tells Madame Michel that she has given her hope again; that truly hearing and seeing Madame Michel reveals to Paloma that "it seems it might be possible to change one's fate after all." (Barberry 2008, 289)

In listening to Madame Michel, Paloma is silently attentive to the suffering of this intelligent, wounded woman. She listens without interruption, and in doing so, a truth, or at least a question seeking the truth, is opened up for Paloma:

> Listening to Madame Michel, I asked myself something: what is more traumatizing? A sister who dies because she's been abandoned, or the lasting effects of the event—the fear that you will die if you don't stay where you belong? Madame Michel could have gotten over her sister's death; but can you get over the staging of your own punishment? (ibid., 290)

There is, of course, an element of self-reflection in Paloma's thoughts. However, reflections on her own life, on coming to understand why she has made this suicide plan (and why now she will abandon that plan), come as a consequence of her silent attention to Madame Michel. Paloma contemplates Madame Michel's life in just the manner of attentive looking that Simone Weil situates at the heart of learning and teaching: "The soul empties itself of all its own contents in order to receive into itself the being it is looking at, just as he is, in all his truth" (Weil 1977, 51). In this passage Weil is referring to the truth of the sufferer (as Paloma receives the truth of the suffering Madame Michel), but she does not limit the objects for our receptive attention to just suffering human beings. Receiving what there is that lies outside of us requires these same dispositions and orientation: "[A]ll our thought should be empty, waiting, not seeking anything, but ready to receive in its naked truth the object that is to penetrate it" (ibid., 49).

Reverence too is not delimited to a narrow range of objects. Neiman is correct in pointing out that "You can have reverence for God or nature, but also for ideals of justice or beauty or truth" (2009, 243). Weil points to "emptying," a "waiting to receive." Neiman tells us that reverence cannot be commanded (although it can be encouraged and I hope to suggest some ways in which it can be done so in classrooms in the next section), and Annie Dillard writes, "But there is another kind of seeing that involves a letting go. When I see this way I sway transfixed and emptied." She goes on to express her deepest desire "to look well at the creek"; a desire that can be achieved only if "You don't run down the present, pursue it with baited hooks and nets. You wait for it, empty-handed, and you are filled" (1998, 33; 104). Weil, Neiman, and Dillard are not suggesting that we become "empty-headed," that we cease to think and feel, cease to be embodied beings moving through the world. Rather, each in her own way is telling us that receptive attention, reverence, and seeing mean first that we behold what lies outside of us and be open to seeing and listening to what those "objects" reveal.

It is not surprising that all three writers introduce humility into their perspectives. Letting what there is in the world speak for itself does demand so great a degree of quieting the self. While many people might consider reverence as solely or primarily a virtue confined to the moral realm, Lorraine Code insightfully suggests an intimate relationship of moral and intellectual virtue:

> Intellectual virtue is, above all, a matter of orientation toward the world, toward one's knowledge seeking self, and toward other such selves as part of the world. Central to it is a sort of openness to how things are: a respect for the normative force of 'realism.' This attitude involves a willingness to let things speak for themselves, a kind of humility toward the experienced world that curbs excessive desire to impose one's cognitive structuring upon it. (Code 1987, 20)

McClintock was open to letting corn speak for itself. Such openness exposes us, renders us vulnerable, not as a weakness, but as a condition for what Anne Carson sees as Socrates's central argument, "that you keep your mind to yourself at the cost of closing out the gods. Truly good and indeed divine things are alive and active outside of you and should be let in to work their changes" (Carson 1986, 155). Neiman recognizes that reverence too is a matter of letting go when she writes, "Like love, it overwhelms you, and if moments of love and lovemaking can be reverent, it's because you know you're in the grip of something vaster than you are"

(Neiman 2008, 245). Beholding what lies outside of us is to allow ourselves to be "transfixed" by something that is not us.

What I have tried to do in this section is point out that the kind of reverential silence I am arguing for is not inward turn to oneself but instead a looking (or listening) outward. Paloma tells us that her sister Colombe is deaf to the value of silence because "her inner space is as chaotic and noisy as the street outside." We live in a society that is committed to never ceasing motion and bedazzled by whatever speeds those movements up. We are seemingly enthralled by the din of the modern world and desirous of carrying it with us wherever we go (I continue to be puzzled by the people who walk and run on a greenway trail in my town "plugged-in"). An environment of constant motion and ceaseless noise is not conducive to reverential silence, not an environment hospitable to becoming gripped by something larger than ourselves. Reverential silence requires, if not absolute stillness (although we oftentimes can see only when we are still) at least something more akin to the pace of walking than high speed Internet. Can these conditions and this reverence be established and nurtured in classrooms where learning and teaching occur?

Fostering Reverence in the Classroom

Annie Dillard's *Pilgrim at Tinker Creek* remains a wonderfully rich description of the virtues of silence in our lives. In Dillard's hands such silence not only quiets and opens up inner space but also renders us receptive to the world around us:

> Can I stay still? How still? It is astonishing how many people cannot, or will not, hold still. I could not, or would not, hold still for thirty minutes inside, but at the creek, I slow down, center down, empty.... I retreat – not inside myself, but outside myself, so that I am a tissue of senses. (1998, 203)

This emptiness is not mindlessness, or even a complete absence of consciousness and thought. It is, however, a kind of passivity that stands opposed to the noise and busy-ness of our everyday lives, to the ways in which we willfully move about filled with and surrounded by that din. The acuity of perception that Dillard has for the natural world and that she invites us to develop as well is not morally neutral. With Dillard we are invited not to look to nature for what is there for us to control and use. She invites us to open our eyes, to look with wonder and awe, recognizing a reality that has value and worth that is not grounded in the acquisitive self. At the same time her pilgrimage at Tinker Creek invites us to see our significance and meaning in connection with—a part of, not apart from—that beautiful and oftentimes cruel world of praying mantises, butterflies, frog-sucking water bugs, and parasitic wasps. An instrumental stance toward the natural world is blind to this way of seeing and experiencing, blind and deaf to the value of such attunement to nature.

For years now I have read this book with doctoral students in an educational leadership program; they are asked to read it over the summer before beginning their doctoral studies. This is done deliberately in the hope that the reading will be done slowly and in fact a number of students remark on just this phenomenon: Dillard's style and the content do not permit a quick read. At the same time they are puzzled by the selection, questioning its relevance, its "usefulness" for them as students in a doctoral program in educational leadership. They recognize that Dillard is describing a way of being in the world that is quite different from their own. The vast majority of these students are busy professionals, teachers, school principals and assistant principals, and central office personnel. They are immersed in environments and work that place priority on control and prediction accomplished as quickly and efficiently as possible. Many, however, are drawn to the way of living and seeing that Dillard describes, recognizing something that is either missing or distorted in their working lives. As Dillard herself is pulled by and then held by the wonder of nature, *Pilgrim at Tinker Creek* draws the reader in, providing an opening for becoming as lost in her prose and descriptions as Dillard is lost to what she sees. On the other hand, they understandably and justly ask: What do the descriptions and meditations of a woman living alone by a creek in Virginia's Blue Ridge have to do with teaching and learning? What, in other words, is worth the good of silence and solitude in a world of schooling, commerce, and consumption that seems to value neither, and in which the busy-ness of my own life does not provide the time or space for quieting the noise, for seeking by way of silence.

One answer to this set of questions resonates clearly and strongly in reading Kathleen Hill's short story, "The Anointed." "In Miss Hughes's seventh-grade music class, we were expected to sit without moving a finger or foot while she played for us what she called 'the music of the anointed" (Hill 1999, 79). Thus the twelve-year-old unnamed narrator invites us to join her in Miss Hughes's music class and to ponder as the story unfolds just what Miss Hughes teaches on those Friday afternoons in her classroom. The narrator tells us that Miss Hughes's class follows a routine: a short introduction about the music they are going to hear followed by Miss Hughes placing the needle on the spinning record, a time during which the students sit quietly and listen (Miss Hughes too quietly stands, puts on her "mask" and listens). If someone shuffled in her chair or broke the silence with a sigh, Miss Hughes would lift the needle from the record and wait "until the room was silent before beginning again" (1999, 79). We learn of Miss Hughes's expectations early in the story and many of our students are initially put off by her enforcing of a particular "posture" while the music is playing; they see the expected stillness as unnatural and see Miss Hughes as imposing some kind of arbitrary restraint on her students. There is the suggestion that the narrator (and her classmates) do at first experience Miss Hughes's expectation in just this way—the invitation to stillness and silence is uncomfortable—but over a short period of time the experience comes to be felt and evaluated differently: "We had just listened to Bach's Fugue in G Minor, for the purpose of learning to recognize the sound of the oboe—and the room for once had an air not of enforced constraint, but of calm" (1999, 81).

What unfolds through this story—and for the narrator her educational transformation is through the subtle interplay of Miss Hughes's music class and her reading of Willa Cather's *Lucy Gayheart*—is the rich and complex living out of the teaching and learning of what Margret Buchmann calls "the moral discipline of quietly receptive attention" (1993, 159). As readers we see a teacher who embodies and nurtures reverential silence in a classroom; a reverence that encompasses both receptive attention to music and to students (specifically attentiveness that is directed toward a classmate of the narrator's, Norman de Carteret—whose estranged father commits suicide—by both the narrator and Miss Hughes). The stillness and the silence we learn are not arbitrary restraints on students, but rather necessary conditions in order to hear, see, and resonate to what lies outside of us, whether that is a piece of music, a fellow human being, or (as Dillard tells us) a muskrat swimming in Tinker's Creek. Early in the short story, as well as early in fall semester in which Miss Hughes is teaching this music class, she shares with her pupils something that they will come to understand only over time: "We go to sleep at night, we wake in the morning, we blink twice and our lives are over. But what do we know if we do not attend?" (Hill 1990, 80). The object for "attend" is deliberately omitted by Miss Hughes, inviting her pupils and us as readers to ask: "Attend to what?" Miss Hughes answers this question through her teaching. First, she follows her call to attend by describing to her pupils her audition to gain acceptance to Juilliard and study under a renowned pianist. She chooses to play Chopin's "Polonaise in A-flat," and tells the seventh graders, "I was so carried away by the fire of the music that I forgot the teacher, I forgot the audition, I forgot everything except the fact that I was now the servant of something larger than myself" (Hill 1999, 80). She tells the class she was afraid prior to sitting down at the piano. Her fearful self is silenced by letting go, letting the music overwhelm her. In asking for stillness and silence before listening to the music she plays in class (the narrator tells us that Miss Hughes, before putting the needle down on the spinning record, "usually asked us 'to silently invite our souls in order to prepare for the journey ahead'") she is asking that they be open to truly listening to the music playing. The stillness and silence are the conditions for letting these students know, in returning to Neiman's words that "you're in the grip of something vaster than you are."

My students (and other readers) begin to see that the quiet passion Miss Hughes has for music—a passion she is sharing with her students—is characterized by a kind of openness and receptivity to the music. They begin to see that this orientation or attitude can also be taken toward math, biology, or history. They begin to see and understand that the subjects they are learning and intending to teach, the human achievements in the arts and sciences, are not bits of information simply to be mastered and controlled, but represent worlds that can evoke wonder and be approached with reverence and as a consequence seen (or heard) in all of their richness and complexity. In this way, they begin to see and understand what Albert Borgmann tells us is a necessity in our hyperkinetic and noisy modern world: "a recovery of the world of eloquent things" (1992, 7).

They see too that the students in Miss Hughes's class do not produce anything; they sit quietly and listen to the music or at story's end they and Miss Hughes quietly turn their attention in the classroom to a grieving Norman. On a Friday afternoon, six days after Norman's father drowns himself in a reservoir, we are shown in a seventh-grade music classroom what Simone Weil calls a miracle, "the capacity to give one's attention to a sufferer" (1977, 51). In the hallways that day before entering Miss Hughes's class the narrator and her classmates either painfully ignore or awkwardly gawk at Norman. Inside Miss Hughes's classroom we see a transformation, one that Miss Hughes has been nurturing for months. A reverence for music unfolds into reverence before a suffering classmate. A playing of Chopin's "Fourth prelude in E minor" sets the stage for potentially transforming the students' perceptions of Norman. After listening to this prelude, Miss Hughes stands silently before Norman, who now has his head buried in his arms resting on the desktop. As the narrator describes, "For a long moment she stood before us, impassive, mouth pulled down at the corners, eyes closed. When she opened them they rested darkly on Norman's lowered head. She allowed them to remain there a few seconds, taking her time, as if she were inviting us to consider with her which words she might chose" (Hill 1999, 88). Miss Hughes deliberately invites the class to truthfully look at Norman, to see with her not a pariah but a suffering human being, a sufferer who should neither be ignored nor gawked at and gossiped about, but seen with a reverence that sees Norman (and I would add sees Norman's dead father) "in all his truth." This truth includes as Miss Hughes goes on to tell the class oftentimes "We cannot see into the mysteries of another person's life...We have no way of knowing what deaths a soul has sustained before the final one...[Yet] I tell you this so you may not forget it. We may honor many things in life. But for someone else's sorrow we must reserve our deepest bow" (Hill 1999, 89). This compassionate attentiveness is possible only when we can quiet our minds; quiet both the external and internal noises that crowd our minds rendering us both blind and deaf. Nurturing an attunement to music and to suffering in reverential silence before both, Miss Hughes is not dispensing information, not even teaching a class in musical appreciation as that term is commonly understood. Instead, she is moving herself and her pupils toward a "recognition of the beauty and suffering that shimmers in the beings of the world" (Farley 1996, 13).

I believe, as it is clear through a careful reading of Hill's short story, that Miss Hughes is a reverent teacher in the sense that Woodruff describes:

> Great teachers listen because of their great passion for learning. Reverent teachers are in awe of the truth, they care about it...even as they know they are more expert than their students on their subjects. But at the same time they are fully conscious of their own limitations. They don't think themselves to be in full possession of the truth. They know they cannot be in awe of something that they think belongs merely to them. (2001, 197)

Miss Hughes remains in wonder and awe before the music she plays, notwithstanding the number of times she has heard the pieces. I believe the same is true of her compassionate wonder before the suffering Norman. In both cases she "knows" more than her seventh-grade pupils, but she never conveys an attitude of omniscience; she continues to seek the truths of music and human suffering through silence and silencing. She is not only a reverent teacher, she is—to return to Woodruff—a "silent teacher": "The silent teacher truly respects students, not because they are who they are. What lies behind the teacher's respect is devotion to truth, and it is devotion to the truth that, at this moment, draws teachers and students into the circle of mutual respect" (2001, 203). When Miss Hughes speaks after silently contemplating a grieving Norman, she says "we would like you to know that you are sitting in the company of friends" (Hill 1999, 88). She knows that no one is Norman's friend; this is an invitation to join a circle characterized by compassionate and truthful seeing. I think it is also unmistakably true that Miss Hughes includes music in that circle of friends. In this way, this reverent and silent teacher enfolds pupils, subject matter, and herself in a passionate embrace of truth.

The students in my teacher education and educational leadership classes are not mean-spirited or insensitive. But as I noted at the beginning of this chapter they are busy; they live and breathe in a noise-filled environment. Silence in their lives and in the classroom makes them uncomfortable. They need, however, an alternative way of seeing learning and teaching in their lives, an alternative to the pervasive instrumental view. Muskrats, praying mantises, music, novels, short stories, and many other "eloquent things." As such they need to be approached with wonder, awe, and reverence in order to be seen. Silence and stillness will allow us to receive the truths of these eloquent things.

References

Barberry, M. 2008. *The Elegance of the Hedgehog*. New York: Europa Editions.
Borgmann, A. 1992. *Crossing the Postmodern Divide*. Chicago: University of Chicago Press.
Buchmann, M. 1993. The Practicality of Contemplative Attention: Devoted Thought That Is Not Deluded. In *Detachment and Concern: Conversations in the Philosophy of Teaching and Teacher Education*. Edited by Margret Buchmann and Robert Floden, 158–173. New York: Teachers College Press
Carson, A. 1998. *Eros the Bittersweet*. Normal, IL: Dalkey Archive Press.
Code, L. 1987. *Epistemic Responsibility*. Hanover, NH: University Press of New England.
Dale, M. 2004. Tales In and Out of School. In *Teaching, Learning, and Loving*. Edited by Daniel Liston and Jim Garrison, 65–79. New York: Routledge Falmer.
Dillard, A. 1998/1974. *Pilgrim at Tinker Creek*. New York: Perennial Classics.
Farley, W. 1996. *Eros for the Other: Retaining Truth in a Pluralistic World*. University Park, PA: Pennsylvania University Press.
Hill, K. 1999, Fall. The anointed. *DoubleTake*, 79–89.
Keller, E. F. 1983. *A Feeling for the Organism*. New York: W. H. Freeman.
Michaels, A. 1997. *Fugitive Pieces*. New York: Alfred A. Knopf.
Neiman, S. 2008. *Moral Clarity*. Princeton, NJ: Princeton University Press.
Shapiro, S. 2006. *Losing Heart: The Moral and Spiritual Miseducation of America's Children*. New York: Lawrence Erlbaum.
Weil, S. 1977. Reflections On the Right Use of School Studies with a View to the Love of God. In *The Simone Weil Reader*, 44–52. Edited by George A. Panichas. New York: McKay.
Woodruff, P. 2001. *Reverence: Renewing a Forgotten Virtue*. New York: Oxford University Press.

4

"Spots of Time That Glow": Reverence, Epiphany, and the Teaching Life

Sam M. Intrator

I always believed that if James Joyce were to write a sequel to *Ulysses*—his sprawling, stream-of-conscious, detail-thick novel that chronicles eighteen episodes in the day of Leopold Bloom—he could write about a teacher moving through a school day. The chaotic style of the classroom life, the enlarged meaning of seemingly humdrum details, and the complex interweaving of different narratives embody the simultaneous, multidimensional context of a Joyce novel. Schools are collections of stories, and teachers are the protagonists in an epic journey of narrative.

Maxine Greene's (1991) observation that at all levels of teaching and learning, "the sounds of storytelling are everywhere" affirms my experience in schools. We understand our practice, our lives as teachers, and our relationship to the institutions we work in through the narratives we tell each other and ourselves. Our stories are essential to our cognitive and affective life and, as Charles Taylor tells us, guide future action by illuminating where we stand in relationship to our commitments so that we can determine "from case to case what is good, or valuable, or what ought to be done, or what [one] endorses or opposes" (1989, 27).

To thrive amidst the stories one must have the capacity to interpret, extract salient information, discern collective patterns, and read contingency. Philip Jackson (1986) contends that teaching "is not so much 'seen' as it is 'read'" (4). In *Teaching: Making Sense of an Uncertain Craft*, McDonald (1992) proposes that view and inquires about teaching as though it were a literary text. Schonmann (1996) compared the classroom episode to a dramatic encounter. Garrison (1997) writes of the *poiesis* of the teaching moment.

If teaching resembles story, then devices that structure narrative provide a useful lens to understand aspects of the story of teaching. One text device that appears in a range of stories teachers tell involves the description of ordinary and routine teaching moments that unfold without fanfare, but then suddenly light up and result in a forceful and clarifying insight into a teacher's practice or provide insight into a teacher's life. This device of storytelling and meaning making was central to *Ulysses* and Joyce's work. The characters in Joyce's works moved through their lives encountering moments that yielded intensive meaning. Joyce's uses of these episodes to structure his works derive from the work of Romanticism and, in particular, William Wordsworth's poetry. Wordsworth evokes the character of these instructive moments in *The Prelude* where he observes, "There are in our existence spots of time, / That with distinct pre-eminence retain renovating virtue" (lines 208–210). It is these "spots of time" that when experienced evoke in us a sense of reverence and wonder for the daunting project of teaching and learning.

For example, here is a transcript of an interview I conducted with a retired junior high school teacher. The interviewee was reflecting on his thirty-five-plus years in the classroom:

> I taught junior high school in Brooklyn for 35 years. I figured it out once: 5 classes a day, 180 days a year over 35 years. That calculates to over 30,000 classes...What is remarkable is how few of those individual classes stand out now that I'm retired. It seems far away, a long time ago, but for half my life—it was my life.
>
> What stays with me? What sticks? Each year, I taught the Gettysburg Address.
>
> "Four score and seven years ago our fathers brought forth on this continent a new nation, conceived in liberty, and dedicated to the proposition that all men are created equal. Now we are engaged in a great civil war, testing whether that nation, or any nation, so conceived and so dedicated, can long endure."
>
> I would look out in my classroom and see these faces. These Brooklyn kids from every country and background and I would well up thinking about Gettysburg and Lincoln and the miracle that is this country. It happened every time I read that speech to them and I would stand there and watch them experience the depth of meaning and relevance of Gettysburg. Lincoln's words would be embodied in my classroom—I could see it in their eyes—with me and my students, "that this nation, under God, shall have a new birth of freedom—and that government of the people, by the people, for the people, shall not perish from the earth." There was so much that broke your back in teaching: know-nothing administrators, kids that

couldn't ever sit still, low status, but then there were these moments. These moments...

"These moments" illuminate the thesis of this chapter: much of teaching is ordinary but amidst the long haul of our classroom work there are "spots of times" infused with reverent wonder, awe, and meaning. Reverberating along a gradient of intensity, some entail momentous insight and mark personal transformation; others can be more modest and evanescent. What is clear is that these moments arrive in "an instant of consciousness, [where] an ordinary object or event suddenly blazes into revelation" (Abrams 1971). To encounter an epiphany means that one apprehends a deep and consequential meaning from ordinary action. Literary critic Morris Beja defines the epiphany as a "sudden spiritual manifestation, whether from some object, scene, event or memorable phase of the mind—the manifestation of being out of proportion to the significance or strictly logical relevance of whatever produces it" (ibid., 18).

The emphasis of this chapter will be on exploring the character of these sudden moments of meaning in regard to teaching. *A teaching epiphany marks a moment of intensified experience in a teacher's practice.* These episodes, experienced in the classroom or in association with our teaching, are both cognitive and emotional and vary in intensity. These sudden insights can illuminate aspects of classroom teaching and our work as teachers that are often fleeting and inaccessible. They provide us with access to the evocative domains of our work.

I begin by exploring the nature of epiphany and how a range of disciplines from theology and literature to cognitive science explain episodes of intensive, sudden meaning. The second half of the chapter interprets a range of interviews and published teacher narratives to propose three categories of teacher epiphany.

First, teacher epiphany involves episodes of *reverence of vocation* where teachers describe an experience that defines their sense of identity as a teacher and their relationship to vocation. These moments represent the "embodiment" of a teacher's most audacious hopes and dreams. Second, teachers often describe spans of time where they feel detached from teaching and tired by the routines of the teaching life. The episodes described in this section, *reclaiming vocation*, illuminate a form of the epiphany that details encounters that revisit our sense of wonder and reverence for our vocation. Third, I will examine how these forms of intense and abrupt insight are integral elements of our practice as teachers. This section considers *craft epiphanies* at a time when teacher development and conceptions of effective practice emphasize logical and rational practice, sudden insight that can inform our practice. Finally, I describe several approaches that strive to cultivate more frequent moments of reverently epiphanic experience.

Versions of Epiphany

While epiphany has come to imply an eye-opening or startling experiencing in modern vernacular, several discrete literatures can inform our appreciation for the phenomenon of epiphanic thought. Etymologically epiphany is derived from the Greek *phainein* to show and the prepositional prefix *epi*, which means variably "on," "over," or "at." *Phainein* can also be translated to mean "to bring to light" and *epiphainein* came to mean "manifest" and "appearance" typically in terms of a literal illumination (Nichols 1987). The essence of epiphany is that one apprehends a deep and significant meaning from an ordinary action or humble observation.

The original idea of epiphany derives from revelatory experiences undergone when one comes to know God. In Christianity, the Feast of the Epiphany celebrates the revelation of God as a human being in the form of Jesus Christ. Across a wide array of religions, the idea of epiphany describes a character of a faith experience when an individual interprets an event as caused by divine intervention.

The Romantic tradition of art and writing elevated the idea of the epiphany as a mode of significant experience that provided understanding and access to vivid experiences that illuminate singular insights into self or the world. Moments can be had that unleash meaning and significance beyond their propositional value. They're often sudden moments of en-lighten-ment, as in entering into the light. The language of the poets embodies this quality of enlightenment. The Moment "gleams like the flashing of a shield," and, as Goethe calls it, a "flash of now." Samuel Taylor Coleridge saw within the world "flashes"; Lord Alfred Tennyson composed much of his poetry about "little things.... that strike on a sharper sense." Wordsworth, in particular, made use of the epiphanic mode to knit together longer narratives by choosing subjects from "ordinary life" that, as Langbaum describe, excite "a feeling analogous to the supernatural by lifting the film of familiarity from our eyes" (1983, 271).

Morris Beja whose analytic work on the modern psychological novel and, in particular, the Irish writer James Joyce whose fiction relied on epiphany as a central element, defines the epiphany as a "sudden spiritual manifestation, whether from some object, scene, event or memorable phase of the mind—the manifestation of being out of proportion to the significance or strictly logical relevance of whatever produces it" (1971,

18). Philosopher Charles Taylor offers a version of epiphany as "a work of art as the locus of a manifestation which bring us into the presence of something which is otherwise inaccessible, and which is of the highest moral or spiritual significance" (1989, 419).

While the epiphany has long been a featured textual structure in poetry and literature, the field of cognitive science has recently begun to develop an extensive research literature examining the qualities of the "aha moment"—a moment that cognitive scientists describe as an episode of insight. Insight is etymologically derived from old Dutch *innsihht,* which literally means "sight with the eyes of the mind." The moment of insight holds mystery for those who strive to understand the neurobiology of understanding, as one cognitive scientist describes, "The suddenness and disconnectedness at which a learner arrives at a solution has caused many people to view insight as an almost supernatural event" (Schilling 2005, 133).

The supernatural quality of these events is linked to the suddenness and its intense emotional quality. As Arne Dietrich describes, "emotions signify biologically significant events, neural activation in emotional structures make for 'loud' signals that are designed to enter consciousness and impress the organism" (2007, 10–20). Once received, the interplay of cognition and emotion results in what Dietrich calls a distinct "phenomenological state" that is referred to as revelation, epiphany, eureka moment, or a religious experience. The yield of this experience is that the percipient feels as though he or she has had a breakthrough that results in the grasping of a universal truth.

A related form of sudden insight has focused on understanding a moment when a solution appears in problem solving. Jonah Lehrer (2008) in an article called the "Eureka Hunt" reports on research by Jung-Beeman who used fMRI and EEG (electroencephalography) testing to scan people's brains while they solved the puzzles.

Although the answer seemed to appear out of nowhere, the mind was carefully preparing itself for the breakthrough. The suddenness of the insight is preceded by a burst of brain activity. A small fold of tissue on the surface of the right hemisphere, the anterior superior temporal gyrus (aSTG), becomes unusually active in the second before the insight. Once the brain is sufficiently focused on the problem, the cortex needs to relax, to seek out the more remote association in the right hemisphere that will provide the insight. As Kounios sees it, the insight process is an act of cognitive deliberation transformed by accidental, serendipitous connections (47).

The researchers describe the brain activity that occurs during this moment as a "binding of neurons" that results in a moment of incandescence. In this manner, the scans that track the gamma rhythms of thought scientifically affirm what the poets describe as the epiphanic moment that asserts that moments can be experiences that unleash both meaning and significance beyond their propositional value.

One of the essential features of the epiphanic involves the highly focused coherence of the insight. It resembles what Dewey (1958) would call a "penetrating quality." Dewey, citing the poet John Keats, refers to the penetrating quality of experiencing a powerful poem as a "spear going through me." What he means is that there's a riveting, singular sense that emerges during intensive experience. Dewey recognizes that while experience is a variegated, multidimensional occurrence the intensive experience requires a controlling focus. Dewey writes that while experience flows as a "thing of histories, each with its own plot, its own inception and movement toward its close, each having its own particular rhythmic movement; each with its own unrepeated quality pervading it throughout" (ibid., 35). This quality is a "single *quality*" (Dewey's italics) that "pervades the entire experience in spite of the variation of its constituent parts" (ibid., 37).

Let me conclude by saying that much of the research focuses on grand insights made by scientists or highly acclaimed artists. The general flow of creative production moves according a process described by many researchers: first, development of expertise and knowledge in a domain; second, idle time alone where incubation happens; third, the moment of insight or epiphany; and, finally, the hard work and elaboration that brings a creative work into the world.

Lehrer (2010) describes an element of this when he writes of wildly productive artists or scientists: "They are epiphany machines, pulling breakthroughs from thin air. Once the epiphany arrives, the artist immediately recognizes its importance, and rushes the idea into paint or verse or melody."

Teachers may also rush the idea into production, but the product is never as tangible as a sculpture, formula, or poem.

Reverence of Vocation

Huebner (1990) calls teaching a "way of living." Teachers are called to the profession by a desire to serve and derive a sense of personal accomplishment and meaning from their work. It is service work, but also work that gives back. As Hansen (1994) explains, "vocation does not imply a one-way subordination of the person to the practice. Vocation describes work that is fulfilling and meaningful to the individual, such that it helps provide a sense of self, of personal identity" (19).

Teachers yearn to feel and understand that sense of worth in their work; however, the practice of teaching can render knowing the impact of one's work elusive. In his essay "The Uncertainties of Teaching," Philip Jackson expresses the difficulty of capturing clear data on our impact as teachers.

> Teachers sometimes have a hard time proving their worth, even to themselves. Why this should be so is easy enough to understand. It derives in large measure from the fact that teaching, unlike masonry or brain surgery or even garbage collecting, has no visible product, no concrete physical object to make or repair or call its own. Consequently, unlike workers in the forenamed and many other occupations, teachers suffer a distinct disadvantage. When their work is finished they have nothing tangible to show off as a fruit of their labor; no sturdy brick wall, no tumor-free brain, no smoothly purring engine, not even a clean back alley to point to with pride as evidence of a job well done. (1986, 55)

Perhaps because the outcomes of teaching are fragile and uncertain we find ourselves attracted to those moments that clarify and crystallize our sense of identity because they embody our ideals. They are as Wigginton (1986) describes, "shining moments." As longtime teacher Larry Cuban describes in an essay "Reflections on a Career in Teaching,"

> In teaching, I have experienced the deep satisfactions of connecting to others in ineffable moments, producing odd tingles, even goose bumps on my back and neck, when a class, small group or individual and I become one—moments listening to students that provided me with insight that upended a conventional idea, moments that forced me to rethink after I had closed my mind's door, moments when my students had touched me deeply. These rare instances are like the resounding crack of a bat that sends a ball soaring into left field or like the graceful pivot to avoid the outstretched arms of an opposing player that allows you to go for an easy lay up. These moments I treasure. (1991, 64)

Or the following, a description written by English teacher Margaret Metzger of "calling in the cosmos" while she's teaching. She illustrates a moment when the cosmos answered her call with an example of the entwined power of pedagogy and subject matter: "Once my class was reading King Lear, and a thunderstorm crashed down just as we encountered the lines: "Blow, winds, and crack your cheeks. Rage, blow." I took the students outside, and we screamed Lear's lines into the storm. I love moments like that!" (1996, 24).

What separates these narratives from much of the empirical literature documenting classroom life is a recurring testimony that vital classroom events unfold within the everyday hustle and bustle of the ordinary. These experiences are often fleeting and subtle. Jackson (1965) once compared the class session to a soap bubble in that its shimmery skin is easily pierced. And the residue from a classroom event, like the residue of a burst bubble, quickly vanishes. These moments embody Wordsworth's notion of "spots of time that glow."

We cherish them because they involve being present when students come to their own moment of sudden insight, growth, or development. The work of teaching can be invisible, quiet, and indistinguishable from the everyday; however, teachers have long described witnessing these poignant and compelling moments. Zajonc provides us a model of thinking about learning as such contends that learning is not imperceptible occasions, but an event that arrives. "Knowledge is an event, a mental occurrence. Teachers, at least good teachers, can tell when it's happening and when not. It is *not* invariably correlated with proper manipulation of equations, or with the perfect performance of a task... Every scientific discovery, then, is a perception of the sort described above, even if its range of validity may prove limited and, in the long run, is superceded by a more far-reaching vision. Likewise, every re-discovery by the student is a cherished moment in education, because in that experience the student relives the same knowledge-event first experienced by a Galileo, Newton, Bohr, or Einstein. In the knowledge-event one touches bedrock" (2000, 4). These are moments when teachers touch bedrock.

Reclaiming Vocation

While teachers strive to find meaning, worth, and value in the work they do as teachers, the research literature describes the difficulty of maintaining commitment to teaching over the long stretch of a career. Almost all teachers go through periods where they are beset and shaken by periods of intense vocational doubt and hurt. Even as they feel competent and efficacious in the classroom they tangle with crucial questions about their ability to sustain their commitment to teaching. The data suggests many school-related factors that are important: overwhelming time constraints, a punishing workload, a sense of loneliness in the work, and the marginal status of teaching.

The reality is that much of teaching is dominated by the grind of everyday obligations, commitments, and vicissitudes. The welter of routines and daily process in schools leave us feeling depleted and akin to what Wordsworth describes in "Tintern Abbey" as a "sad perplexity" of "half-extinguished thought" where "joyless daylight" and the "fever of the world" blunt one's heart and spirit. Dewey's accounting of ordinary experience generalizes that our normal state of experience is deeply lethargic. According to Dewey, "(o)nly occasionally in the lives of many are the senses fraught with the sentiment that comes from deep realizations of intrinsic meanings. We undergo sensations as mechanical stimuli or as irritated stimulations... We see without feeling; we hear but only a second-hand report, second hand because not reen-forced [sic] by vision. We touch, but the contact remains tangential" (1934, 22). Psychologist Mihaly Csikszentmihalyi (1975) likewise depicts everyday experience as being deafened and distracted by informational noise; choked by anxiety, worry, and confusion; marked by the severance of action from awareness; preoccupied with extrinsic material and social reward, and thinly felt because of the superficial, flat concerns that pervade our lives. The central proposition is that routine experience undergone over time can devolve into a ubiquitous flatness. As a third-grade teacher described in an interview,

> Every year, I get to the point where I'm so tired and emotionally taxed that I feel like I can't go forward. I guess every profession has those valleys, but I find this stretch exhausting. Invariably, I refind a spark in a small moment. I get a student who was fragile, but then does something strong like stand up for a classmate. I have a student who was struggling with their writing make a breakthrough. These moments come randomly, and I wish they could come more frequently, but they sustain me.

The essence of this common trope across teacher narratives has to do with "lost vocation" or "recognition of weariness and burnout" and having a pivotal experience that inspires reclamation of vocation.

Robert Kunzman (2002) describes one of these episodes in a narrative titled "The Meaning of Life Assignment." The narrative begins with him describing the frustration he felt teaching *King Lear* because of the detachment students presented. He describes a particular sense of loss teachers feel when they teach a portion of their subject that has deep symbolic and meaningful attachment to their life, but when they share it with students there is no spark or light. He writes, of hoping to see students get excited around the moment when a broken Lear is reunited with his faithful daughter Cordelia and beseeches her, "Pray you now, forget, and forgive. I am old and foolish," and through her tears she insists she has "no cause" for anger against him. Despite the raw and evocative drama that Kunzman felt, his students blithely skimmed over it. In response to his frustration—over this episode and others—he describes his effort to design a different form of response:

> With all these works, we had stood at the edge of this vast expanse of meaning, perhaps even wandered around a bit on the fringes, but it was not really our own in the way that signaled deep engagement and lasting value for our lives. I searched for ways to ask, how do these stories, these insights *move* you? What insights into personal identity and meaning resonate with you? We spend so much time in the classroom—how does any of it connect with what matters most to you? I needed a way to bring our conversations to this place of intimacy and authenticity for all of us. What emerged—The Meaning of Life Assignment, as I grandly titled it—was simple enough on its surface.
>
> *The question is surely as old as the subject: what is the meaning of life?... Your assignment, your challenge, is to answer that question as best you can. We've read and discussed different viewpoints on the issue, and your personal insights, beliefs, and experiences certainly provide your own perspectives.*
>
> I handed students a single sheet of paper with these words and a few more, and told them they could use whatever media and format they felt best suited their responses, and they would share their "answers" with the class in some sort of presentation.
>
> Their reactions varied but struck me as promising. Some were incredulous—and appreciative—that a major project was being devoted to this question. A few, of course, wanted to know how I could possibly grade such an assignment. The most common response, however, was a combination of "this looks really hard" and "I can't wait to get started." I remember one girl returning to the next class in exasperation—the assignment had taken hold of her, and she complained of having done no work for her other classes. I wasn't sure what exactly to expect when presentations began in two weeks, but I grew hopeful that students were starting to move away from the fringes and strike out on their own paths. I wondered whether they would be able to communicate those journeys to the class, and if their peers would truly listen.
>
> I won't forget Jenny's presentation on the first day. A sweet, quiet young woman who rarely spoke in large-group discussions, she began her presentation in a soft, halting voice. "It's kind of ironic that the one day I'm supposed to talk about the meaning of life, I watched someone die," she said. "This year, I've been volunteering some mornings at a hospice before coming to school." Her eyes began to fill with tears. "Today, I sat with a man as he died." With those words our class entered a space we had never experienced together, and my worries about respectful listening vanished. We had been given the gift of hearing a student reflect on this awesome event, to consider connections between our learning that year and the learning in our lives. (Kunzman 2002, 86)

Kunzman describes a quality of the classroom that exists beyond the prosaic language of standards and conventional curriculum. It is a place of raw, intense, awesome human spirit. These moments evoke in teachers a sense of the reverent for what is possible in the vocation of teaching. They are moments Jackson (1992) describes of teaching with "an altered state of consciousness" (67).

Craft Epiphanies

The epiphanic experience also has substantial utility in our practice. The sudden insight into classroom dilemma, a student's nature, and the interplay of subject, pedagogy, and student learning is indispensable. It's a mode of extracting essential insight from the complicated system of the classroom. In a single day an elementary teacher may have more than a thousand interactions with students. High school teachers may have 150 students per day and multiple interactions with many of them. Teachers and other professionals rely on sudden insight to guide their practice because teaching demands immediate thought and action in an unpredictable system where many things are happening at once.

As Hawkins argues in a piece describing the role of epiphanic thought and the practices of physician, "an epiphany is a moment of recognition and revelation... though it may be prepared for over long periods of time, the experience is not gradual but immediate... it is experienced as abrupt and total" (1997, 135–136). She contends that the complexity of the physician-patient dynamic is such that often "flashes of understanding" can be crucial in diagnosis and practice. In relationship to teaching, I want to highlight three forms of epiphanic knowing that shape our work in the classroom.

One genre of epiphany that occurs for teachers involves those experiences undergone in their own learning that illuminate some enduring principle that they carry back into their practice. These flashes of insight often occur when teachers find themselves in the "role of student" while they are teaching. One interview I did with a teacher involved what they learned while taking furniture-making class in their tenth year of teaching:

> I just didn't get it. The power tools intimidated me, the other students in the class all struck me as confident, they had an easy rapport with the teacher, and they seemed to know each other. I was the clumsy outsider and my anxiety shut me down. I couldn't learn. I resented being there and ultimately, I stopped attending. What hit me one day as I was driving home feeling lousy about myself was how here I was an accomplished

adult and yet I was useless in this course. I gripped the steering wheel and all these faces ran through my head—all these young people who passed through my classes who experienced all of what I just described. I resolved then and there to notice these kids and do something more in my teaching.

This episode describes how a poignant encounter outside of school connects leaving an imprint that perceptively shifts a teacher's practice.

Another frequently reported form of sudden insight within teaching has to do with observations that emerge in our reading of the classroom milieu. The teachers that I interviewed described numerous forms of these sudden insights. These insights might be "aha" moments of genuine meaning, which is central to the definition of epiphany; however, they lack the revelatory impact that is unique to epiphanic knowing. For example, here are several teachers describing the quality of these moments of insight:

> Sometimes I'd be framing up directions to the class and I'll look out and I'll read the general tenor of confusion or concentration. It's a moment when you generalize information and draw a conclusion.
>
> I get sudden insights frequently, particularly about specific students. Let me give you an example: the other day I had students writing an essay. I started with the typical mode of asking them to read the question and then I had this "aha"—why don't have them think of themselves as writers. I stopped and said, "Writers write. You are a writer. How do you think writers begin?" We had this really fascinating discussion and we began the prewriting/thinking again and it was so much more meaningful. I get these 'aha' moments all the time.
>
> By way of contrast, one teacher described the experience of discovering a ritual of community that she has become a weekly classroom practice.
>
> It happened on a throwaway Friday. It might have been a day before vacation. I decided that I would find out one thing 'good' and surprising about each student and publicly recognize them instead of the typical do now. I did some information gathering over the week and started class on Friday by asking each student to stand up. They all clapped for each other and I was so moved by how proud and delighted they looked even when they looked embarrassed. I felt the rightness of it while it happened and I knew it was because they yearn for some positive recognition. I knew it was right and I have done a version of this since.

The outcome of this event, as described by the teacher, is a small, but significant change in practice. The epiphany reorients a practitioner's approach to their work.

Cultivating Epiphany

To James Joyce (1956) the epiphanic was the "most delicate and evanescent of moments" and so it was the obligation of the man of letters or the artist to both seek and "record these epiphanies with extreme care" or they would flit by and meanings would be lost. In Richard Ellman's (1982) biography of Joyce he observes that Joyce believed that one must "look for them not among gods but among men, in casual, unostentatious, even unpleasant moments." Likewise, Virginia Woolf implores us to "poke our head" through the "cotton wool" of "nondescript daily life" so that we can experience what Maxine Greene describes as moments of "wide-awakeness." The collective advice is to pay attention because meaningful experience is an achievement. Objects, works of art, text, and experience are, to quote Dewey, "literally pregnant with meaning" (1934, 118). Poignant and instructive meanings about one's teaching can be pursued, composed, extracted, formed, and shaped.

Jackson (1986) hints that there are moments of wonder and drama in classrooms; however, these moments are soft and perhaps indiscernible through traditional modes of seeing classrooms. He urges two adjustments. One he urges us to narrow our vision to allow us to "focus on features of the environment that we might ordinarily pass by—small details and minuscule events, happenings that come and go in a twinkling" (Jackson 1992, 85). While Jackson's first suggestion asks us to focus our angles of vision more minutely, the second entails the temporal dimension of our gaze. Changes—particularly the humble and subtle events—are hidden in the soupy complexity of a classroom. He calls to the Romantic artists like Blake, Shelley and Keats to use as models of "seers" because of their capacity to "see" a universe "in a grain of sand."

Jackson's invitation to bring the habits, spirit, and tools of the poet to our classroom work can be cultivated by engagement with poetry. Azar Nafisi, the author of *Reading Lolita in Teheran,* tells us that when bombs fell around her when she was teaching in Teheran during the Iran-Iraq War she read James, Eliot and Plath, and great Persian poets like Rumi and Hafez because "during such times, when our lives are transformed by violence, that we need works of imagination to confirm our faith in humanity, to find hope amid the rubble of a hopeless world."

Teachers don't face the screech of air raid sirens, but we face a tough, demanding job doing which needs a full, attentive presence if we are going to do the work justice. Teachers struggle to keep their hearts energized, their spirit alive and their integrity intact. Teachers need their soul in the work and poetry as Edward Hirsch tells us is "soul-making activity"

(1999, 31). To this end, poetry too initiates a turn inward. Reading poetry helps us host the conversation that matters most: our conversation with our own dreams, values, and sense of being in the world. Poetry moves you back into yourself, which is the place to begin if we are to capture and make meaning of these soulful moments. As W. H. Auden says, "the primary function of Poetry, as of all the arts, is to make us more aware of ourselves and the world around us."

A second form of encountering the epiphanic can come through a form of professional development designed to examine the vocational terrain and inner life of teaching. One particular approach was founded by Parker J. Palmer as the Courage to Teach (CTT) Retreat. CTT is a program of quarterly retreats for the personal and professional renewal of public school educators. In this program, a cohort group of twenty–thirty educators gather for three-day, quarterly retreats over a one- or two-year period. In large group, small group, and solitary settings, "the heart of a teacher" is explored, making use of personal stories, reflections on classroom practice, and insights from poets, storytellers, and various wisdom traditions. The following shows how this approach addresses the challenges of renewing vocational vitality:

> Twenty-five teachers and administrators sit in a circle, giving their full attention as an elementary teacher speaks passionately and poignantly about her love for her students and her commitment to reach each and every one of them. She goes on to tearfully describe the personal toll this is taking on her own life—creeping guilt at not having enough time or emotional energy to give to her own family, bone-deep exhaustion, nonstop worrying about the safety of some of her students, the weariness of facing an always burgeoning mountain of papers and projects to grade, a sense of increasing isolation from friends and colleagues because there is simply no more to give. The listeners sit quietly, respectfully, as she finishes, each reflecting on their own version of her story. The next teacher speaks of the debilitating effects on the morale of his colleagues as more and more pressure is being placed to raise test scores at his school or else! While teaching was once a labor of love, it is now becoming an onerous task as the nearly singular focus on standardized testing dominates all communications among faculty and administrators. More silence. The next person to speak, a newly appointed principal, describes her recent attempts to mediate an explosive situation between a student, his parents, and a teacher. In the midst of helping the parties work through their threats and misunderstandings, she has become aware of the heavy burden of responsibility she carries. Yet in the telling of her story, she also recognizes a growing confidence and inner sense of authority, grounded not in her role as a new principal, but in her personal integrity. Around the circle it goes—each person relating stories and examples of how their complex journey as teachers and

leaders has unfolded since the last time they were together a few months ago. (Jackson and Jackson, 2002)

As this vignette illustrates, the curricula of the retreats do not focus on pedagogical methods or content knowledge, but on the exploration of personal and professional beliefs. As with many programs focused on supporting adult development, the CTT model invites teachers to voice their own ideas and feelings and explore the meaning embedded in their personal experiences. The dialogue described sought to invite teachers to explore the deep well of their vocational calling and was evoked by a pair of questions.

What aspects of your identity and integrity feel most threatened or endangered by your work? What aspects of your identity and integrity feel most supported and engaged by the work you do? Using dialogue, reflective silence, journaling, and poetry reading, the CTT program invites teachers into sustained examination of questions such as those just suggested. The intense focus on the "inner life" of teachers in the setting focuses attention on the small but highly transfixing moments that are epiphanic, while also reshaping a teacher's orientation toward vocation.

To give the most effective summary of the literary epiphany, I offer a passage from Annie Dillard's *Pilgrim at Tinker Creek*. It begins:

> CATCH IT IF YOU CAN. (Italics added) It is early March. I am dazed from a long day of interstate driving homeward; I pull in at a gas station in Nowhere, Virginia, north of Lexington...I am absolutely alone. There are no other customers. The road is vacant, the interstate is out of sight and earshot. I have hazarded into a new corner of the world, an unknown spot, a Brigadoon. Before me extends a low hill trembling in yellow brome, and behind the hill, filling the sky, rises an enormous mountain ridge, forested, alive and awesome with brilliant blown lights. I have never seen anything so tremulous and live...how can I have not noticed before that the sun is setting? My mind has been a blank slab of black asphalt for hours, but that doesn't stop the sun's wild wheel. (1994, 324)

When Dillard challenges us to "catch it if you can," she captures the essence of the epiphany. It's always there to be caught. Amidst the most banal and ordinary circumstance, one can have an experience that can be momentous and significant of the spiritual and the aesthetic. Our teacher's minds are often described as the equivalent of the "black slab of asphalt." However, as Dillard conveys, the mundane pulses with the sublime. Dillard's refrain is to "catch it if you can." When you do, nothing can seem so "tremulous and live."

Again, it is my contention that within the raucous press of classroom life there are experiences that resemble geodes, those rocks of most ordinary texture and shape that when cracked gleam with intricate, infinite patterns of crystal. I have characterized this moment of gleam as a reverent epiphanic encounter and argued that this literary form appropriated from the Romantics can help us appreciate its qualities.

References

Abrams, M. H. 1971. *Natural Supernaturalism: Tradition and Revolution in Romantic Literature.* New York: W. W. Norton.

Beja, M. 1971. *Epiphany in the Modern Novel.* Seattle: University of Washington Press.

Dietrich, A. 2007. Who's afraid of a cognitive neuroscience of creativity? *Methods* 42 (1): 22–27. doi:10.1016/j.ymeth.2006.12.009.

Dillard, A. 1994. *The Annie Dillard Reader.* New York: HarperCollins.

Ellman, R. 1982/1959. *James Joyce.* Second Edition. Oxford: Oxford University Press.

Garrison, J. 1997. *Dewey and Eros: Wisdom and Desire in the Art of Teaching.* New York: Teachers College Press.

Greene, M. 1991. Foreword to *Stories Lives Tell: Narrative and Dialogue in Education.* Edited by Carol Witherell and Nel Noddings, ix–xi. New York: Teachers College Press.

Hirsch, E. and Duke University. Center for Documentary Studies. 1999. *How to Read a Poem : And Fall in Love with Poetry.* New York: Harcourt Brace.

Jackson, P. W. 1986. *The Practice of Teaching.* New York: Teachers College Press.

Jackson, M., and R. Jackson. 2002. "Courage to Teach: A Retreat Program of Personal and Professional Renewal for Educators." In *Stories of the Courage to Teach: Honoring the Teacher's Heart.* Edited by Sam M. Intrator, 282–307. San Francisco: Jossey Bass.

Joyce, J. 1956. *Epiphanies.* Buffalo, NY: Lockwood Memorial Library: University of Buffalo.

Kunzman, R. 2002. Meaning of Life Assignment. In *Stories of the Courage to Teach: Honoring the Teachers Heart.* Edited by Sam M. Intrator, 84–94. San Francisco: Jossey-Bass.

Langbaum, R. 1983. The epiphanic mode in Wordsworth and modern literature. *New Literary History* 14: 335–358.

Lehrer, J. 2008. THE EUREKA HUNT: Why do good ideas come to us when they do? *New Yorker* July 28, 40–45.

———. 2010. "David Galenson," *The Frontal Cortex* blog, February 22, 2010 (6:46 p.m.), http://scienceblogs.com/cortex/2010/02/david_galenson.php.

McDonald, J. P. 1992. *Teaching: Making Sense of an Uncertain Craft.* New York: Teachers College Press.

Nichols, A. 1987. *The Poetics of Epiphany: Nineteenth-Century Origins of the Modern Literary Movement.* Tuscaloosa: University of Alabama Press.

Schilling, M. A. 2005. A "small-world" network model of cognitive insight. *Creativity Research Journal* 17 (2): 131–154. doi:10.1207/s15326934crj1702&3_2.

Schonmann, S. 1996. The culture of classrooms and the problem of policy in the making: The case of the ugly duckling. *Arts Education Policy Review* 97 (4): 18–23.

Taylor, C. 1989. *Sources of the Self: The Making of the Modern Identity.* Cambridge, MA: Harvard University Press.

Wordsworth, W. 1850. The prelude. In *Romantic Poetry and Prose.* Edited by H. B. and L. Trilling. Oxford: Oxford University Press.

5

Awakening Reverence: The Role of Descriptive Inquiry in Developing Perception and Reverence—The Case of the Prospect School Teacher Education Program

Carol Rodgers

Introduction

This chapter investigates how teachers develop the capacity to see students and their learning, when seeing is understood as going beyond and beneath noting the surface aspects or factual details of people and things, and reaching toward a more deeply felt connection. Seeing, or what Dewey (1934) refers to as "perception," I argue, grows out of a disciplined attention to the world, and can, I posit, lead to "reverence." Such disciplined attention can be cultivated by processes collectively identified as "descriptive inquiry" (Rodgers 2010; Kesson, Traugh, and Perez 2009; Himley and Carini 2001; 2010). Based upon a phenomenological research paradigm, and drawing largely upon the work of Merleau-Ponty, these "descriptive processes" were first developed by Patricia Carini and her colleagues from 1965 to 1991 at the Prospect School, located in North Bennington, Vermont, and continue to evolve through the various institutes, conferences, and publications that trace their origins back to Prospect. In 1968 Prospect took in its first graduate students of education. Interns, as they were called, studied and student taught at Prospect and local schools for the rest of Prospect's existence. I take a close look in this chapter at the learning of one of the graduates; I will call her "Annie" of the Prospect School Teacher Education Program, and her development of the capacity to perceive her students with awe, wonder, and humility, and the elements of reverence contained therein.

The primary argument I make here is that the descriptive process developed at Prospect and practiced by its student interns cultivated a capacity for perception that, in turn, opened space for an feeling of reverence that fits the definition of reverence Rud and Garrison propose in their Introduction to the present volume, though the word "reverence" was never used by the graduates nor the faculty of the program in either the documents I examined nor in their interviews. The descriptive process, including descriptive inquiry, will help us better understand why they say that detecting "reverence can be more a matter of moral and imaginative perception than cognition." Certainly, that was the case for Annie. They attempt to detect reverence in some brief statements by Codell and Stephanie (as cited by Rose). I wish to do the same for Annie in a more detailed and precise manner using descriptive inquiry.

Garrison and Rud derive their understanding of reverence from Woodruff (2001). The focus there is on wonder, awe, and respect, and on feelings of human limitation and even shame. While I instinctively recoil from the concept of shame, calling forth as it does the act of shaming others, which is so closely tied to children's painful experiences in school, I do find evidence of exactly this emotion in Annie's story. Feelings of human limitation are also present and align with Carini's own stance. When faced with the complexity of a child or a child's work, she admits that "the subject of my attention always exceeds what I can see. I learn that when I see a lot [e.g., in a child's piece of work], I am still seeing only a little and partially" (Carini, 2001, 163).

Following a discussion of my theoretical framework, and a description of my methods, I will explore a journal entry made by Annie, an intern at the Prospect School Teacher Education program and the ways in which description, perception, and reverence were at play in her inquiry into the learning of one student.

Theoretical Framework: Description, Perception, and Reverence

The theory that frames this study has been derived from Patricia Carini's (1979; 2000; 2001; 2010) writings on description and descriptive inquiry and John Dewey's writings on perception. In my discussion of reverence

I draw upon my own sense of the word, as well as on Rud and Garrison's notions of reverence in this volume, and David Hansen's (2004) concept of a poetics of teaching. I see these three core elements—description, perception, and reverence—as interrelated in a causal way, where the practice of description hones the capacity for perception, which, in turn opens up an internal space for reverence.

Description

I have written elsewhere of the role of description in reflection (Rodgers 2002a; 2002b; 2010). I see the act of description as part of a larger cycle of reflective thought that both precedes and includes "intelligent action." Dewey distinguishes intelligent (considered) action in contrast to routine or habitual action (Dewey 1933; 1938). Likewise, Carini, in her essay "On Seeing and the Visibility of the Person," writes on one hand of the usefulness of habitual ways of seeing (which every teacher recognizes as critical to getting through a day), but, on the other, its dangers and attendant "evil." Carini writes:

> In its most benign form, habituated perception is reassuring and indeed useful.... But, there are limitations and implicit dangers in habituated perception.... When habituated perception is carried to an extreme of circumstance (e.g. extreme physical need), or through a failure to exercise the gift of vision (e.g. ordinary "busy-ness"), the world may come to be seen only from the frame of reference of person need. Then both the viewer and viewed are impoverished, detachment replaces interest, and the world loses its power for calling forth meaning. (1979, 11)

On a very straightforward level, description stands in contrast to interpretation. For example, one could look at a child's painting of a flower and sun and immediately label these elements as "sun" and "flower" or describe each using language that takes into account what is actually there: a yellow circle painted with several brush strokes that seem to move from the outer edge to the inside of the circle, located in the upper, slightly left-of-center portion of the paper. And "flower" might require many separate descriptions to get at all the elements that are present. In both cases, the act of describing enables the seeing. It is in the practice of having to name what one sees that one learns to see intelligently.

In addition to forestalling interpretation, description provides evidence—warrants—upon which further analysis and interpretation are based, and from which action is taken. To be able to describe requires of the describer that she or he be open to experience. The more open, or present, one is to experience, the more one takes in, and the more one has at hand to describe. In other words, the longer one holds at bay conclusions about what one sees, the more one sees, and the more one sees, the more evidence one has to work from to draw complex, multilayered conclusions. In this way one remains "open to what is not yet imagined" (Kesson, Traugh, and Perez 2006, 1864).

On a more profound level, description requires discipline of the describer. First it requires that he slow down. The desire to label and categorize what one sees and thereby to draw conclusions about it so that one can quickly "move on," is deeply engrained in teachers who must attend to, manage, and "cover" so much simultaneously. To take the time to actually *see* can feel like "wasting" time, so it also requires a commitment to the value of seeing even in the face of pressure to keep moving. It also requires a willingness to look closely at one's own assumptions and an acceptance of one's own limited knowledge. The reward, as Carini suggests, is that such patience and discipline then make room for a thing (or person) to become "fully present." She writes poetically of the process:

> Describing I pause, and pausing, attend. Describing requires that I stand back and consider. Describing requires that I not rush to judgment or conclude before I have looked. Describing makes room for something to be fully present. Describing is slow, particular work, I have to set aside familiar categories for classifying or generalizing. I have to stay with the subject of my attention. I have to give it time to speak, to show itself. (2001, 163)

Detecting reverence, or having a reverent experience, often requires providing time for the subject to speak to us, to show itself.

Description may be done in isolation, but comes to fruition only when done in the company of others. As Carini says, in learning to describe in the company of others, we learn that each of us sees the world only partially, and we need others to approach a "fuller" description: "I learn that when I see a lot, I am still seeing only a little and partially. I learn that when others join in, the description is always fuller than what I saw alone" (ibid., 163). There is at least a hint of reverent humility here that arises from the comprehension of our human limitation that Rud and Garrison reference.

Phenomenology focuses on the particulars of lived experience, and description is its primary methodology. At Prospect, the experiences that mattered were the lived experience of students as seen through their work and their actions in the world as well as the lived experience of teachers.

Kesson, Traugh, and Perez, in their article on the contemplative nature of these descriptive processes, describe this methodology:

> Phenomenological educational inquiry focuses on the act of perception, and the detailed description of that perception...Description is the core methodology of [Prospect's] phenomenological inquiry. (2006, 1969)

In my own work with teachers and reflection, I found that it is this patient act of description that is often the hardest. The desire to name the "problem," fix it, and move on is strong in teachers. It is also engrained in our nation's own psyche. We look for evidence long enough to confirm our own preconceptions (witness our contemporary "culture wars") and then dig ourselves deeper into the ideological holes we inhabit. It indeed demands "a disciplined, rigorous effort," to see the world "profoundly and authentically."

Perception

John Dewey, in his seminal work, *Art as Experience*, writes movingly about the character of perception, contrasting it with the act of mere "recognition":

> The difference between [perception and recognition] is immense. Recognition is perception arrested before it has a chance to develop freely. In recognition there is a beginning of an act of perception. But this beginning is not allowed to serve the development of a full perception of the thing recognized. It is arrested at the point where it will serve some *other* purpose, as we recognize a man on the street in order to greet or to avoid him, not so as to see him for the sake of *seeing what is there*. (Italics added, 1934, 52)

Reverence involves remarkable perception. Because reverence initially involves vague feelings of awe and wonder that in themselves are unnamable, we may never merely recognize it. Descriptive inquiry can help us detect such reverent moments in teaching better than other more exclusively cognitive, interpretative forms of inquiry. It allows us to perceive Annie's reverent perception and the practices of Prospect School that cultivates such perception along with many other types of profound teaching that other research methods would miss.

Too often, we stop our inquiry, our reflection once we have a label we feel fits. It allows us, Dewey says, to move on. Perception, in contrast to recognition, is the result of both "a disciplined, rigorous effort to understand experience profoundly and authentically" and time. As Dewey writes, "in no case can there be *perception of an object* except in a process developing in time" (ibid., 175). This effort is the effort of engaging with—*and staying with*—the object of one's perception. It involves an interaction between the perceiver and perceived that can change both. It is a rhythmic and dialectical affair.

Dewey asserts that the result of this process is appreciation. Appreciation involves both an intellectual and an emotional valuing of the object of perception; the intellect and emotions "come together and unite" (ibid., 277). This union of intellect and feeling is characterized by a sense of "aliveness" on the part of both the artist and the perceiver of art, where there is "active and alert commerce with the world" and "a complete interpenetration of self and the world of objects and events" (ibid., 19). Reverence requires such perception.

Reverence

In the context of teaching and learning at Prospect, reverence in teaching (as opposed, say, to reverence in nature or other contexts) arose from a focus on children (physical appearance and gesture, strong interests and preferences, connections with others, disposition and temperament, and modes of thinking and learning) and children's work. It is grounded in their complexity and capacity as human beings, in our essential relatedness, and in the particulars of their everyday experiences. One powerful metaphor for reverence in teaching is what David Hansen (2004) calls a "poetics of teaching" where the teacher is moved by and responsive to the expressiveness of the child's commerce with the world. Said differently, a poetics of teaching is about a teacher's presence to the human becoming of his students. It presumes that education is about becoming more human and humane, toward oneself and others, and seeks, through this process, to extend this humanness, thus adding value to the world. It suggests a stance that is alive to the expressiveness of each and every human being as well as the expressive nature of the world itself. It recognizes that when perception is alive, a teacher is emotionally *moved* to respond. It recognizes that it is our commerce with the world, and our inexorable need to express it, that weaves our humanness into existence:

> This process of active response to the world, involving a deepening understanding and sensitivity, mirrors how events, actions, and the conduct of others...A poetics highlights this relation between world and person: on the one hand, how the world is expressive, and, on the other hand, how persons come to "read" that expressiveness. (Hansen 2004, 122)

Why does this matter in teaching? Quite simply, if we assume that we are educating humans into being, it matters that we attend to the human beings whom we educate. It matters that we perceive and respond to the expressive selves that are the only selves who learn, that is, who take the world (plants, paintings, numbers, sky, language, architecture, history) into themselves, make it a part of their selves, and who, in turn, re-create the world they perceive and making themselves a part of it, and it a part of themselves. It matters that we are "moved"; otherwise we would not act.

These selves—our students' and our own—are all we as teachers have to work with. We are all, as Carini says, "poets of our lives," constructing, as we live, both ourselves and the world in a "sustained and powerful dialectic" (2001, 20). To have the right to say that we have taught and that students have learned demands that we touch this expressive center of the learner that seeks to make meaning of, and to make meaning*ful*, the world. As Hansen writes, it is our moral obligation to "[support] in every way possible each human being's growth, while [also drawing] from each human being the best that he or she can provide to others" (2006, 168). Perceiving human potential as well as poetically actualizing it can require reverence.

The School, Its History, and Its Philosophy: A Brief Overview

The Prospect School was cofounded in 1965 by Patricia Carini, her husband Lou, and two other parents as an alternative to the more traditional schools of the small Vermont town in which they lived. The Prospect School Teacher Education Program was initiated in 1968 and continued until the close of the Prospect School in 1991. Prospect's philosophy had several intertwining roots: the lives and works of children, the phenomenological perspective of philosophers Maurice Merleau-Ponty, the educational views of John Dewey and Alfred North Whitehead, and the everyday experiences of teachers at Prospect.

In the beginning of Prospect's history, in an effort to better respond to the children in their care, Prospect teachers and staff searched for ways to know them better. Because of the choice-based, emergent curriculum that characterized Prospect, they found themselves with massive amounts of children's work, from paintings to writing, to block constructions to sewing projects. So, they decided to begin by looking closely at children's work. "Bound up in the making of works," writes Carini, "are the maker's gestures and expressiveness, her ways of engaging the world from the angles from which she sees it.... A child's works map a path to what the child values, strives for, holds to as expression of self. In brief, works mark a path to the child's self-making" (Himley and Carini 2010, 155–156). This move shifts the focus of attention "from how the child is seen by others to what she herself expresses more or less unmediated by others' perspectives" (156). With insight into the child's "self-making" the teacher was able to respond with suggestions, activities, questions, situations, and resources that offered possibilities to simultaneously extend the self, deepening and broadening his or her knowledge of the world.

As the processes of observation and description of works became more and more refined, Prospect's repertoire of descriptive processes grew (and continues to grow today). They grew organically, out of the work of children and the needs and questions of the Prospect staff, and also deliberately, as an outgrowth of Carini's own background in phenomenological research and profound philosophical grounding. It is relevant to note that the research that Prospect conducted was laced with a kind of reverence for the capacities of the child—of all human beings—to express their selves in the process of creation. To watch and aid a human in the process of becoming is an awe-inspiring (if at times aggravating!) endeavor.

The full meaning of this for Prospect is beyond the scope of this chapter, and is represented extensively in writings that have emerged from the work there (e.g., Carini 1979; Himley and Carini 2000; Carini 2001; Himley and Carini 2010). What seems essential to say here is that value was placed on the primacy of experience and expression, and on the need to see the particulars of each. "For it is in the particularity of what is attended to," writes Carini (echoing Merleau-Ponty and Hansen), "that courage to move on to the next step and the next [in teaching] is found. It is particularity that sets aside reliance on ready-made solutions, that nurtures poetry and a poetics of educating" (2001, 124). We now move to the particulars of Annie's experience.

Annie's Work with Kelly

Annie, who came from a Catholic working-class family in the Northeast, had already taught for two years in inner-city Philadelphia when she decided to "make the trek to Vermont" to study. Her passions included reverence for social justice causes, particularly in the political arena (protesting the war in El Salvador and supporting the revolution in Nicaragua). While teaching in Philadelphia she met "the women" from the Philadelphia Teachers Learning Cooperative (the PTLC), a Prospect-inspired study group that continues today, and they had taken her under their collective wing. In this section, we will look at what Annie learned from working with one of her students whom I will call Kelly. The year was 1986 and Annie's first teaching placement was in a third-grade public school in a rural town in southwestern Vermont. Being Vermont, the school was virtually all white with a mixture of socioeconomic groups, though the children came from largely working-class families. There were about twenty of them in the class. In response to a long-term assignment to observe and describe their experiences, Annie kept a daily journal. The journal was handwritten in a lined, bound notebook in Annie's flowing calligraphic script. She was passionate about Ireland and the script had a sort of Celtic, artistic character to it. What follows is one excerpt among many, many similar ones, from that journal that provides evidence of Annie's learning at Prospect, namely, evidence of her capacity to describe, her skill at perceiving Kelly's learning and Kelly's desire to express herself in the world, and Annie's own sense of both awe and humility in the face of Kelly's humanity. In this excerpt Annie describes her work with Kelly as Kelly figures out how to tell time, reconciling her prior learning to what Annie is trying to teach her. (All errors, punctuation, and original notations have been left as is.)

Journal Entry

Thurs. 2 Oct [c. 1986]

Going over pg. 39 in math w/ the kids while Bea called Library....
Most knew it—recognizing—on the hour—time on the clock (ie 8:00, 3:00) Introducing this ½ hour time seemed to be a review for most as well.... Donald and Crows (Charlie, Todd etc) rush through papers like these
Kelly didn't have pg. 39. So I took the large play clock over to her desk (while others were working) to review with her by moving the hands.
The O'Clocks (8, 9, 2, 4 etc) she knew—right off.
"See I'm not dumb. I know this, it's easy."
Acknowledging all that, I went on to the ½ hour bits, there Kelly was calling 1:30, 2:30 and 2:30—3:30 etc. My first reaction was to say in that benevolent dictator way, no, Kelly, this is 1:30 not 2:30. But Kelly <u>insisted</u>, absolutely insisted, that it was 2:30. The <u>verve</u> with which she told me this sort of jolted me and I stopped telling her and began asking her questions in an effort to see how she was arrived at such a conclusion with such conviction (and just to note for myself—Kelly's strong sense of herself, which some teachers will label as arrogance, came through in her insisting. This woke me up and made me realize, again, why it is I have made this trek to Vermont—to be actively listening and perceiving all I can in the classroom.) I think of what the most likely reaction might have been of most kids and I think of politeness, deference, obedience to authority etc... as

influencing the response or lack thereof.... I was telling her the right answer. I must note every time I have this dulling of my perception.

However, when I realized what was happening I stopped talking and wanted to hear Kelly. I wanted to record it all, word for word, in my head (in order to reflect upon it later) and here's the closest approximation to it.

I then turned the hands to 2:30 and asked her what time it was. She said 3:30—because it was past the 2, closer to the 3—The small hand. The big hand was on the 6, which meant 30. I tried different times (6:30, 9:30 etc) in order to see if this logic was constant—if there was a pattern to her thinking. Throughout this time, I was almost overwhelmed by her insistency. She kept on saying that Ms. Cane (her kindergarten teacher) taught her this and taught her it this way. What startled me I guess, was her injured look in her eyes, as if she was about to cry. This is a child who can appear to be very callous where, whether things bothered her or not, she would often give the air of indifference. She has been in 3 different foster homes, wears a hip brace that causes her to walk slowly from side to side etc... When I came into the class, it was obvious that she held her own w/ the other children, was not intimidated by them. The other 2nd graders (boys included...ie Todd etc) I think, are a bit overwhelmed by her. She's very sophisticated. Needless to say, the honest, near-teared eyes, made me stop and rethink this stereotype that I had allowed to build in my mind. Oh, I was always warm and kind to her, but I was not being as cognizant of Kelly's feelings (and I know the depth of feeling an 8 year old has) because, on the surface, they weren't very visible.

Then, later in the day Bea mentioned to me that "I wonder why Kelly insists on not hanging her coat up." There's that word again. It's a clue to what Kelly's all about.

The simple exchange with Kelly left Annie full of reverent wonder and awe as well as respect and humility.

Discussion

A close reading of Annie's entry reveals a good deal about her learning at Prospect, especially in regard to her capacity to slow down her natural urge to react, describing and reflecting not just after the fact, but in the moment, her forcing herself to perceive, in Dewey's sense of that word, what Kelly was up to, and her respect for her humanity, as well as her own sense of humility and awe in the face of Kelly's strength. In the next few pages, I go into detail, drawing upon the analysis done through two collaborative close readings of the excerpt.

When Annie writes, "My first reaction was to say in that benevolent dictator way, no, Kelly, this is 1:30 not 2:30. But Kelly insisted, absolutely insisted, that it was 2:30. The verve with which she told me this sort of jolted me and I stopped telling her and began asking her questions in an effort to see how she was arrived at such a conclusion with such conviction" we see a number of shifts of awareness. Annie was "jolted" by the insistence in Kelly's voice from a stance of "benevolent dictator" to a curious observer and inquirer. Caught up short, Annie suddenly shifted from telling—dictating— to listening. The task shifted from fixing something that was wrong in Kelly, to seeing her as a person with the capacity to make sense of her world. How had Kelly arrived at her understanding? Annie also feels the power of being "told" by Kelly—this is a meeting of equals now, rather than a knower and a learner. Kelly has a voice, her full self is present in this moment, and she "insists" this self into the picture. Notably, rather than insisting on asserting her power over Kelly, Annie steps back and takes note. Not only was Annie curious to know how Kelly made sense of clock time, but, more importantly, where—from what part of her—Kelly's insistence came.

"This woke me up," writes Annie, as though she had been asleep to the person of Kelly and her sense-making. She was now conscious of—present to—this child who would not play the expected role of "student," "polite, deferent, and obedient." This causes Annie to reflect on her own role as "teacher." She reminds herself again of why she made this trek to Vermont— "to be actively listening and perceiving all I can in the classroom." This sentence could well serve as Annie's mission statement. Her journal is our evidence—and hers—that she can do this. She is noticing, *and noticing her noticing*. She affirms its goodness and alignment with her mission, declaring her commitment to being a learner, and underscoring the need to avoid the "dulling of her perception" that telling (versus perceiving) can cause. She has a growing awareness that questions can open a vastness of possibility that telling simply cuts off. With telling there is no learning. With listening and asking one can find the way to understanding. She thus sets a high standard for herself, one based in social justice—not being a dictator, but someone who makes space for the voice of the less powerful, a child. She senses that perception allows Kelly to be seen, and that this is morally right.

In this passage Annie reproaches herself—"I must note... this dulling of my perception"—conveying as Garrison and Rud (2009) put it, a sense of shame at her own impulse to silence Kelly's insistence on being heard, being seen, cutting off what Hansen calls the expressiveness of the child.

Remarkably, Annie is able to stop herself in mid-telling (reflection-in-action) and attends to an awakened desire to "hear Kelly." One could equally say here, to "see" Kelly and who she was. At this point Annie's actions shift from showing to inquiring. She experiments, setting a number of different times on the clock (2:30, 3:30, 9:30, 6:30) to see what Kelly would say, gathering evidence "in order to see if [Kelly's] logic was constant—if there was a pattern to her thinking."

Throughout this episode Annie is "almost overwhelmed" by Kelly's insistence that her kindergarten teacher had taught her to tell time this way. But she also is "startled," taken aback, by the "injured look in [Kelly's] eyes, as if she were about to cry." This touches Annie, moves her. She has the insight that Kelly, who has in the past Annie had occasionally thought of as callous is, perhaps, not. She entertains the possibility that Kelly's insistence, rather than indicating callousness or indifference, in fact, denotes deep caring and "depth of feeling." By asking instead of telling, Annie created space for Kelly to be, and to be seen. What was "on the surface" gave way to feelings and understandings that had been invisible.

At the end of her journal entry, Annie returns to the word "insists," and begins to think that perhaps this is a "clue to what Kelly is all about." The word "clue" suggests that Annie has, by the end of this reflective passage, set out to know Kelly, and will continue to look for clues. While we don't know the resolution of the time-telling lesson, we do know that by its conclusion, she sees Kelly more fully, differently, as more complex, more human, with a sense of self and her own fierce but vulnerable intelligence. We also see Annie changed, more humble, more committed to Kelly, clearer about her own role as inquirer rather than teller and more aware of Kelly's complexity as a human being. As David Hansen puts it, "The teacher is affected by signs of grace, harmony, and beauty-in-action, as well as by indices of frustration, rupture, and breakdown. In other words, the teacher is moved by the concrete revelation of human being in students' gestures, words, and deeds" (2004, 132). As noted earlier, one powerful metaphor for reverence in teaching is David Hansen's notion of a poetics of teaching. You can see that metaphor at work here.

Flash Forward

Twenty years later, I interviewed Annie to see what had endured from these early insights into teaching and learning. Annie describes the work she was now doing with teachers. It is remarkable how her words echo this early journal entry:

> I try to listen. I try to, try to listen and restate. I try and understand what they're saying. I try not to judge, first and foremost. And you know, sometimes I say some pretty outrageous things and you know it's hard. I mean it's really important for me to try not to judge. [...] A lot of that stuff about assumptions, attitudes, prejudices, all of that. And a good deal of my work is unpacking these kids. And it's really, I can tell you, it's like practicing psychotherapy without a license, in many ways, because it's more about where [teachers] *are*, *who* they are and how they can accept other people.

And you know a lot of that work has to be done before you can even be open to seeing what children have to offer. And it's so, this is the big, this is, this is *it* in my work.

She illustrates this work with an example. The student of one of the teachers she has been working with, Tyrone, was someone who had trouble staying seated. Annie explained how she worked with the teacher:

> I asked her some probing questions about, you know, why do you need for him to sit? And what are you looking to accomplish? And could that happen with him standing? Do you think he would be happier standing or sitting? She was able to answer all of that and see that. And, in that way I'd say she's a quick study. She really is. But she's usually, you know, doesn't get on him to sit. So in that way I try to help her to see each kid as the individual person that they are.

Similarly, as with her work with children, Annie looks for strengths in the teachers with whom she works. She tells the story of James, a new teacher teaching in an inner-city school where it's difficult to find teachers. He had a hard time with classroom management—one visit from a supervisor saw a desk being thrown in her direction. Annie thinks the administration would probably have gotten rid of him if there had been anyone they could find to take his place. But Annie and her two mentor partners chose to focus on James' accomplishments and small victories.

> So, it's interesting because a lot of the conversation between Rhonda and myself, and Ina too, in that trio, in relation to James was around: let's work with his strengths and see what he *does* present and what he *can* do and all of that, because there's a whole ball of what he can't do—in terms of the situation that he is in.

The day that I interviewed Annie, she had a meeting with the other mentors and when they discussed James' work they noted that he was using one of the strategies they had taught. Annie jumped to her feet shouting, "Look at the growth! Look at the growth!"

At the end of the interview Annie talked about "tapping into that deeper river within me." It is, perhaps, here that I come to the heart of Annie's experience at Prospect. She talks about working with the teachers in the mentor project, and refers to her use of "transparent facilitation" and presence—her word. When I try to get her to describe what she means, she speaks of two things—first, a sort of walking your talk, doing what you are asking your learners to do, something that teachers at Prospect did with children and with interns; and two, being present, which seems to mean really listening, being fully oneself, and *being* the thing one is teaching, rather than "phoning it in," which seem to me like more than just "walking your talk." It's closer to fully embodying your beliefs, a total fusion of theory and practice, mind and body, praxis:

> I guess the transparent facilitation label, or catch-all phrase, that taps into that deeper river within me that comes from Prospect, is about just really just being present and being real. To be, to be transparently facilitating you really have to put it out there. And the teachers at Prospect were very present. [Carol: What do you mean by that?] They, they weren't phoning it in, so to speak. They were engaged in the *practice* of teaching kids and listening to kids. When I was in Andrea's room and we were doing this Wild West theme, we were all in the Wild West. We were *living* in the Wild West. So, then, you know, in conversation with David,...he was very present to me in the conversation. So I guess the piece about transparent facilitation is that notion of presence. That, I think, is what taps into the Prospect experience. [...] David kind of modeled for me without telling me that, you know what—it's really good if you can get the kids to do stuff with their hands. You know, don't just talk to kids about bridges, let kids build bridges and then talk to kids about bridges. Pull it in together. In relation to teachers, don't talk to teachers about constructivist curriculum, *do* it. You know, *be* it—in the more general sense.

The "being real" Annie refers to can be traced back to her reflections on Kelly where she vowed not to "dull her perceptions" and to allow the "real" Kelly a space to be, as Carini says, fully present. Van Manen writes: "Whoever gives a gift (and not just a mere present [from a store]) gives himself or herself. He or she *is* the thing" (1990, 115). As Annie said, "You have to *be* it [what you are teaching.]" Teaching this way is, then, is a "gift." Being present is making of oneself a gift to another. Prospect did this for Annie and Annie did it for Kelly, and now does this for her teacher-learners, working with them to do this for their kids. Paying it forward.

Conclusion

This chapter relies on three interrelated concepts: description, perception, and reverence with the hypothesis that cultivation of the first two leads to the third. Annie's story, as embodied in both her journal entry made during her time as a teacher intern at Prospect, and her interviews, twenty years later, show evidence of her capacity and commitment to describe in detail the learning and the emotional response of her learners. Not only was Kelly's thinking drawn in detail, along with her physical and emotional responses, but so were Annie's *own* thoughts and feelings and assumptions. Prospect's focus on description and its commitment to a phenomenological philosophy and view of human beings "in the making" laid a path for her our emerging awareness, and, as Dewey *calls* it, "intelligent action." As she said in her interview, at Prospect, "you've got to stay with an idea, you know, work with it, ... not mak[e] assumptions or tak[e] shortcuts in your thinking.... It was important not to get sloppy." In other words, it was important to see what there was to see, to take that time to gather the particulars so that one's perceptions were not blunted. Annie's description of Kelly was of a complex human being, a child, not narrowly conceived according to standards and norms, but broadly *perceived* as a person, knowable. As Carini writes,

> The person, from this [non-reductionist] viewpoint, has intrinsic value, and his or her being and experience have both coherence and durability— that is, integrity. The person from the viewpoint is knowable, understandable and educable through his or her choices. (1987, 11)

And yet they are also mysterious because they are always becoming. The reflective discipline of descriptive inquiry laid the foundation for *perception*. With Kelly, this was possible once Annie discarded her stance as "dictator" in favor of that of questioner/inquirer and listener. This opened a door, putting her *in relationship* with Kelly. Once one sees the "other" it is inherently a two-way deal. One opens oneself, as Annie does, to being moved and thereby changed, by the other. This shift that Annie makes, as inquirer and relationally, opens the possibility for learning to occur.

From a Deweyan perspective, Annie moved past "recognition"— "Ah! This is a problem of not understanding how to tell time on the half hour!"—to perception: the history of Kelly's (mis)understanding, the need to be seen as "not dumb" that lay behind her insistence, the need to be seen as a person with thoughts, feelings, and a voice, rather than an obedient and compliant student. Annie in the space of her story began to see the things that were not "visible." Dewey writes that when we begin to perceive a person "[w]e realize that we never knew the person before; we had not seen him in any pregnant sense. We now begin to study and to 'take in.' Perception replaces bare recognition" (1934, 53). Years later, as evidenced in her interviews, Annie retains her capacity for perception and her valuing of those with whom she works. Clearly, these were not just exercises she did in graduate school, but transformations that endured.

Finally, while Annie never uses the word reverence in her interviews or journal, it is clear that she feels something akin to it. It is true that she came into the program with a reverence for truth and justice. However, it is clear that these commitments were significantly expanded and refined at Prospect and through the processes she engaged in there. She says:

> [When I came to Prospect] I was very involved in, you know, protesting the war in El Salvador and supporting the revolution in Nicaragua. You know, so I was pretty out there. And this was—I guess what I was hearing, at Prospect, was a much more subtle but wider—it wasn't constrained by mere politics. There was a philosophy that I was attempting to understand; it was much larger than any one—much larger than just the constraint of where I was coming from, the politics, the political stuff.

Reverence opens itself to the experiences of humility, shame, and respect; we saw Annie's early experience with Kelly as reflective of both. In being "taken aback" and "startled" by Kelly's insistence and depth of feeling, she conveys a certain shame of her initial impulse to rush through the lesson without taking into account who Kelly was. And as she slows herself down in the moment to observe Kelly more closely, then, later, to describe what she has seen, staying with it long enough to perceive who Kelly might be, she develops a respect for Kelly's strength, compassion for what she has been through, and recognition of her (Annie's) own "human limitation." As Garrison and Rud note,

> We are interested in the larger ideals and values of teaching, such as a reverence for the lives of students, actualizing students' full potential, dedication to self-transcending...care and compassion for students, and commitments to the truth of what we teach. Teachers who revere these and other ideals of their profession will feel shame when they fail to live their lives according to the values. (2009, 2637)

It is my contention that, as Annie Dillard writes, "What you see is what you get" (1998, 17). The first step, I believe, is educating teachers to see the particulars of students' (and their own) experiences. One's perceptions determine one's experience of the world. If we work to enlarge our perceptions, as Annie did, what we get is complex, awe-filled, wondrous, and humbling, and worthy of our reverence.

References

Carini, P. F. 1987. *The Art of Seeing and the Visibility of the Person.* Grand Forks: North Dakota Study Group.
———. 2001. *Starting Strong: A Different Look at Children, School, and Standards.* New York: Teachers College Press.

Dewey, J. 1934. *Art as Experience*. New York: Perigree Books.
Dillard, A. 1998. *Pilgrim at Tinker Creek*. New York: Harper's Perennial.
Garrison, J., and A. G. Rud. 2009. Reverence in classroom teaching. *Teachers College Record* 111 (11): 2626-2646.
Hansen, D. T. 2004. A poetics of teaching. *Educational Theory* 54: 119-142.
Himley, M., and Carini, P. F. 2001. *From Another Angle: Children's Strengths and School Standards*. New York: Teachers College Press.
———. 2010. *Jenny's Story*. New York: Teachers College Press.
Kesson, K., C. Traugh, C., and F. Perez, F. Descriptive inquiry as contemplative practice. *Teachers College Record*, 108 (9): 1862-1880.
Rodgers, C. R. 2002a. Defining reflection: Another look at John Dewey and reflective thinking. *Teachers College Record* 74 (4): 842-866.
———. 2002b. Seeing student learning: Teacher change and the role of reflection. *Harvard Educational Review* 72 (2): 230-253.
———. 2006. Experience as art: The process of valuing and appreciating the work of children in teacher education. *Teacher Education Practice* 19 (4): 434-454.
———. 2010. The role of descriptive inquiry in building presence and civic capacity. In *The Handbook of Reflective Inquiry*. Edited by N. Lyons, 45-61. New York: Springer.
Rodgers, C. R., and M. Raider-Roth. 2006. Presence in teaching. *Teachers and Teaching: Theory and Practice* 12 (3): 265-287.
Van Manen, M. 1990. *Researching Lived Experience*. Albany, NY: SUNY Press.
Woodruff, P. 2001. *Reverence: Renewing a Forgotten Virtue*. New York: Oxford University Press.

6

Risking Reverence

Elaine J. O'Quinn

From the first day I stepped into a classroom as a teacher, I knew that any moment spent teaching in ways not relevant to the lives my students and I were living was to dishonor us both in some profound way. Our shared mortality insists on something bigger than the rhetoric that defines school. From controlled power structures to impositions of limits, I have continually found myself puzzling through a system that allows little opportunity for reverence, reflection, revelation, or creation. Because it abhors weakness, public education approaches the most vulnerable in all of us as something to be minimalized rather than named and explored. What is sacred is not the human condition but human capital. Humility, awe, and wonder are in short supply; ironically, so are honor, duty, and respect. Possibility means test scores, and knowledge is associated with mastery rather than discovery.

As an educator, I understand that my role goes beyond the organized activities of classroom life. I have learned that life outside of class continuously spills into the community teachers and students co-create. Bits and pieces of what constitutes who we are and what goes into our personal making cannot be filtered or separated out from the dynamics of educational activity. When they are, it becomes too easy to ignore the intricacies of evolving self-knowledge and self-worth. The complex work of teaching includes taking risks and learning to listen not only to intuitions, but also to the articulated expressions of others. It requires consideration of how mind, body, and spirit are inextricably bound and recognition of the subtle but gracious joys that underpin daily interaction with students. Teachers must acknowledge their failings as much as they do their successes to improve the conditions of education and move forward in humble understanding of the complex work we do. Anything less is a mockery.

Starting from Silence

Students enter the classroom as I write across the board "ONCE YOU READ THIS, PLEASE REMAIN SILENT." I am wondering what they will make of my words. They are used to teachers telling them what to do, so I assume they consider this another rule to follow. One by one they drift into the space we will share for the rest of the year, some seeing the message straight away, others catching on only when they notice friends falling silent. Soon, all are curious and still, looking for a sign of what the words mean. My smile throws them. They are not sure what to trust. Fingers to my lips, I establish that I wish them to come with me, to enter the empty halls. Wary but willing, they rise and we go. *(Risk is good, a small voice reminds me. Risk is good.)* They are fragile, but so am I, and any potential for honest community is dependent on a reciprocal acknowledgment of that fact. Respect is something we both must give and earn.

As we move down the steps, my thoughts begin to drift. (I'm thinking of those teachers for whom I'd have done anything, teachers [so trusted, I knew they'd never do me harm] who [unknowingly?] revealed me to myself. I want so badly to give something of that to my students.) For a moment, we stop on a landing and listen. Only the short ring of an office phone and the distant laughter of cafeteria workers can be heard. No more shuffling feet. No whispered giggles. The students have started to settle. In the quiet, they dip into their centers. ("From the center," says the Tao, "all things take their course."). It seems enough to trust the adventure. As we continue to walk, some students fall into pairs, others move alone or in small groups, and each stop we make becomes its own little world. The steady pecking of keyboards at the computer lab, the scan and pitch of the office copier, and the hum of voices are a backdrop to the business called school that is taking place. I think of Whitman and his poem "Who Learns My Lesson Complete?" ("I lie abstracted and hear beautiful tales of things and the reasons of things, They are so beautiful I nudge myself to listen."), and I wonder what it is my students hear in our silent space. I study their youthful faces and see remembrances of unforgotten pleasures and unbelievable griefs. Together, we continue to make our way.

Early on, students hear a plea to take school seriously for the sake of their future, in order to be somebody, for a successful life. Clichés assail them. Education is a journey ("Race to the Top"); a ticket to a brighter tomorrow ("No Child Left Behind"); a chance to shine ("Authentic Assessment").

From the ringing of the bells to the sounding of the standards alarm, they are led to believe the classroom is a testimony to the value of their labor and discipline, an inspiration to insight and self-discovery. But for many (if not most), the promise falls short. Bodies are seen as vehicles rather than messengers, and the excitement and experience of the student's natural state is cancelled out. The journey becomes less a search for oneself and more a quest for the truth of others, a push away from the center of self to the self-centered replication of what is deemed knowledge. Frivolity, play, and even honest affection are generally discouraged, replaced with sterile slogans, an endless sameness, and a false sense of what matters. What is revered is that which is reticent and deliberate. Reflectivity and even creativity are perceived as threatening and rebellious, because to know the world for oneself is to imagine it differently from what others may deem acceptable. Industry, not imagination, and limits, not possibilities define the traditions. Attending to anything more is to risk disruption of the status quo and the methodical structures of the culture of school. Knowledge anticipated as a flight into the mystery of being is quickly revealed as a prison of calculated rules and ordering.

April 20, 1834
The whole secret of the teacher's force lies in the conviction that men are convertible. And they are. They want awakening.
—Emerson

The garish caw of a crow reminds me it is time to start back toward school; reluctantly, I stand as a swell of warm August air blows through the stand of trees *("In the woods is perpetual youth,"* claims Emerson) and across the splashing creek *("Who knows but these may be the lessons fit for you?"* echoes Whitman). No motion, no expression at all is needed to stir my students to their feet; one by one, they join me. As we get closer to the building, someone shouts from an open window. Jack-hammers can be heard breaking apart a road a few blocks away, and the steady beep of a construction truck backing up reports loud and clear. A dog barks across from the main parking lot, and as I open the door, a woman yells at him to be still. The sound of school smacks us full force as we step inside. My students seem visibly taken aback. As they quietly find their seats, a sense of something important seems to take hold. *(Listen to the silences within.)* Our "play" takes on new meaning. They watch as I walk to the board and write under my earlier message words that I hope will serve them well in our time together:

The Path of Things Is Silent
—Emerson

Just then, the bell rings.

Journal Entry: I took a risk today that opened my students to the possibility that something different could happen in English. I'm anxious to see how they respond. I want them to learn they can think differently about our little world of school. I want them to trust themselves in ways that foster their growth, not stifle it. I want to change the rules. I must learn to be the fool.

Teaching dependent only upon the perceived actuality of what we call school can be threatened by new ways of seeing. When innovation is assumed only as a way to fill a particular need or serve a certain end rather than allow for abundant ways of creation, the mystery of our abilities to learn dissipate. Traditional ways of knowing insist upon learners who believe only experts can teach what there is to learn. Students have little opportunity to know the world through themselves. Instead, they come to believe that their creative natures must be defined through what are deemed identifiable experiences. I am not speaking here of the virtue that exists in learning about the practical and mundane. I am referring to the thoughtless and cramped "one size fits all" way of conceptualizing the world. This limited means of self-exploration is censorious and disparaging. Based on productivity rather than creativity, such an approach erases the actual wonder of learning. "Seeing schooling small" (Greene 1995, 11) presents students in a negligible light. It dishonors them in ways that negatively impact the learning community. What should be reverence for individual uniqueness is pathologized into the limitations of imperfection.

When the paper reflections come in from our walk, I am struck by the sincerity, strength and richness of them. Almost everyone reaches deep and offers a thread of connection. John wishes for a quiet place of his own. Rita remembers what it is to hear her own voice. Lonnie finds peace. Cassie notes how one silent moment allows her to open her feelings to difficult memories. The responses are not at all what I expect. I learn firsthand that shadows of every shape and size surround our students, and I realize I must allow for that, honor it in some way. Personal discouragements, unavoidable road blocks, and sudden miseries blanket them, follow them through the day. I see that sorrow, pain, and confusion are no less real for them than they are for me (*"Sorrow makes us all children again,"* [I recall Emerson.] *"destroys all differences of intellect. The wisest knows nothing..."*). So that we may grow our community, I know I must brace for their pain and recognize too my own despairs. Already, I have a changed notion of what I value in my students. They are as vulnerable as I am. Why did I expect anything less?

Journal Entry: Responses to yesterday's lesson weren't what I expected. I'm exhausted by the voices that tell me students can't and won't do what the "standard" considers to be enough. What do they know? I want my students to rail against such insinuations, to passionately believe in their worth, to work hard to make sense of who they are and what their lives can be no matter what anyone says to the contrary. I want them to make meaning for themselves, despite the discomfort it may cause. I want them to understand that knowledge does not have to be a prison and that the unendurable alongside all that is wonderful will be acknowledged in our class.

("Ms. O'Quinn, please come to the office." My father is gone. "Ms. O'Quinn." Now too my brother.)

Connecting Body, Mind, and Soul

It is early one spring when I notice how skinny Randall Miner has gotten. His complexion is that pale translucent color that tends almost to blue. I have been spending time with him, trying to help prepare his financial aid form for college next year, so I know he is living on his own in a fairly rough part of town known for its share of street alcoholics and hardcore drug users. Randall has been denied independent status by the financial aid offices where he has applied, and we are trying to figure out how to make the officers believe he really does live on his own. My phone calls to them are almost comical, always resulting in "we need to talk to his parents." They do not seem to get that if they could talk to his parents, he would not be filing for independent status.

At the moment, however, I am more concerned about Randall's health. I know he has struggled with alcohol use in the past, and I worry that his situation has pushed him to return to his old habits. Anxious about how he is surviving in such an adverse environment, I ask how he is managing to stay afloat. He thinks I mean financially and quickly tells me he has been selling his plasma on a two-week cycle in order to eat. I am ashamed that my first thought about his poor physical condition was so judgmental. He smiles and asks if I have a made any headway in helping him acquire independent status. I am humbled by Randall's ability to accept the dire circumstances of his present situation while maintaining an innocent trust in a system that in the end will ignore his incredible spirit.

(*Randall never makes it to college. He doesn't get the money. Instead, he joins the army. He has tears in his eyes the day he comes to say goodbye. It's the last I hear from him.*)

Because we are physical beings, we cannot live in the world without experiencing it through our bodies, though school, to some degree, would have us ignore our physical experience. In his work on moral imagination, Mark Johnson talks about cultural metaphors of action (1993). Citing the work of George Lakoff, Johnson reports the findings that indicate that a physical metaphorical mapping defines how people understand the ways they get to particular destinations in their lives. Bodies and place are the launching pad for much, if not most, of what happens to us. Unfortunately, the processes of schooling generally ignore the importance of studies like Lakeoff's.

(I see George hiding out in the back corner. From behind my big teacher's desk, I watch him move his smaller seat to an angle that keeps him out of sight. Ninth grade. Plenty of time already to learn how to fade into a null existence. Day in and day out, he arrives, moves his seat, and stays out of range. He is poor, has trouble at home, knows how to melt away, evaporate while remaining in place. School is an ironic refuge.)

Instead of recognizing the vast differences that exist among students, a regimented, lock-step approach to understanding them prevails. Expecting a common experience too often results in consequences that are out of rhythm with the uncontrollable realities of the rest of life. The result is that many students are set up for failure before they ever get started. It is only by respecting that students' daily lives cannot be separated from their school lives, by accepting the implications to their abilities and capabilities brought on by their genuine conditions, that we can expand and honor rather than limit and judge the whole of their experiences. Only through synthesizing existing conditions with imagined subsequent ones can we come to open understandings of what we might do to help students achieve something of personal value. Not doing this means that many students go through school without ever being validated in the lives over which they have little say or control. If their lives are not validated, they simply become invisible.

(Patricia Darnell is missing. Each day her empty desk grows larger and larger until it threatens to ravage the whole room. "Sandy Ridge girl," some whisper in the teachers' lounge. "Loose," declare the boys. "Drugs. Short skirts. Too much makeup. Party girl." [Her desk swells in size and pushes us breathless to the walls.] Quiet. Often silent. Quiet and still. Very still. I remember her. The year passes; no trace. Only the dry bones of her name remain piled in the corner of our classroom, arid sticks of human driftwood severed and scorched by a brutal, disapproving sun.)

Crystal begins crying in class one day in the middle of a discussion about Jamaica Kincaid's book, *Annie John*. We are talking about Annie's relationship with her mother and about what the kids think makes for good parents. Crystal's parents abandoned her when she was younger. *(There is risk, I remind myself. Getting beyond it is crucial.)* As the tears drop softly to her chest and brutally stain the purple shirt she wears, I walk over and quietly excuse her to leave the room. Silence, tender and malleable, stays behind. I look around the room and find that even Josh, who makes a joke of everything, is still and stares hard out the window. "I'll be back," I say. "Talk quietly while I'm gone, or work if you prefer. I'll be back in a few minutes." A couple of students take out their notebooks. Some put their heads down. Others turn in their seats. But Josh still sits and peers hard out that window. I go to Crystal, but part of my heart remains in the room, open and breaking for Josh. Sorrow comes in many forms. I have learned my kids are no stranger to its nature.

(I enter the school to find students crying in the hall. Tommy Wilson has died. Tommy. My God, he was so sweet and funny and kind. And tall. Tall like his father. Tall and kind and funny and sweet. I can't go to the funeral. I just can't. It's weeks before I can, one warm spring day, gather flowers from my yard and take them to his grave. Gently, I lay them on the uncaring ground where his warm smile is forever at rest, and I sit and tell him how much he taught me about my own life. Tommy, so tall and funny and ever kind. I, too, am the student here. I am.)

Journal Entry: It's difficult talking with students about feelings and relationships. Bringing the personal into the public is taboo. A colleague told me I shouldn't use the word "love" when talking about my students, that "love" should be reserved for family. But today, I tried to pull wide the door that Annie's mother's character opens up. The tendency is to slam it tight. Bodies and the relationships they stand for don't exist at school. Still, I could tell that my students want to understand Annie's relationship with her mother. It's not knowledge of the text they want to pursue; it's self-knowledge. It's hard to speak to each other about these things because there's enormous responsibility in listening to the personal. I notice the students constantly observe what I share, how I hear what they say. It's tough work. Sometimes in wonder, sometimes in horror, we pause and reflect and turn a thing over until satisfied we have given credence to it in our deliberation. It's the way we move forward in the most painful of things. I am learning how to be a bridge.

("Ms. O'Quinn, I'm sorry about what happened in class yesterday. I thought I could talk about those things better. I'm okay. Everyone was nice to me afterward. Nobody tried to get in my business. Reading the book just made me think more about people's lives. I'm okay."—Crystal)

To have reverence for our students means contemplating the whole of their existence, not just what is most convenient or comfortable to know.

We must recognize that there are layers and connections to what we pursue with them in the classroom that cannot be predicted. *(Risk is always present.)* Like it or not, we are constantly crossing back and forth between the meanings being made of lived experience and the stories being told. We cannot grow without the intimacy that comes only when thinking about and acting within the indivisibilities of life that embrace us all. This is not the same as growth that merely accommodates or is glossed over with a veneer of objectification and disassociation, of this I am certain.

Similarly, reverence for the essence of what it means to teach requires a recognition of the entire experience of it. It means believing that the very best of what our students are and what we are rises out of us only after reflective consideration. It means striving for integration and trusting that out of such unions will come meaningful insight into the realm of possibilities that exist for us as individuals and as a people. Mostly, it means acknowledging that teaching is a highly personal experience that falls flat when reduced to method and manner or split into technical halves. To revere our work as teachers means to live in the knowledge that we touch others only when we allow ourselves to be touched. It is only by "attaching," says Michelle Fine, "what is to what could be" (1992, 225) that we authentically, imaginatively invite students to write the indelible chapters of their lives.

Waltzing with the Muses

I am furious with my ninth graders because they will not read the Steinbeck novel I have chosen. They think it is boring and irrelevant. Only a handful will read. I try to reason with them. I threaten. I bargain. But things do not get much better. In desperation, I give daily quizzes, assign two-page essays, all to no avail. In the end, I simply sit them down and read them the story. *(Practice patience.)* I paint with the author's words a picture of Kino and his family. They become curious that phrases and symbols can become a living emotion. I ask them to tell personal stories that speak of lessons equally important. We stumble, but regain our ground. Now the students cannot deny the lure of such simple characters, so different, yet so similar to who they are and what they too sometimes feel. They talk about their own dreams and what they are willing to give up to get them. They tell of times when they too lost sight in the short term of what makes life important in the long run. *("The results of life are uncalculated and uncalculable. The years teach much which the days never know."—Emerson)* Together, we decide to make papier-mache pearls that hang from the classroom ceiling in lustered orbs, beaded pieces of the moon. On the string that holds them, each student attaches a statement of a personal dream. Like celestial jewelry, the pearls drop pale and shiny across the sky of our room. For years, I let them hang there, a reminder of my own youthful dreams. "In every life," writes Louise Gluck in her poem "Presque Isle," "there's a moment or two" (1993, 49). (I am thankful for mine.)

Teachers use the tools of their discipline in a variety of manners to further student growth. Each chooses a very different path. In retrospect of my own way, I recognize that the intimate nature of my approach is not executed in an attempt to assimilate students. Through refusal to separate the personal from the public, I endeavor to strengthen their connections to the world. Through reflective sharing, I bid students to distinguish and refine the differences between living deep and living shallow. *(Recognize illusion.)* Reading and writing are mere links that allow for the conversation of our thoughts to take up arms, ask for the comfort of them, or understand better the urgent need to extend them. In this way, I hope that the wonder and revelation of things are not lost or quickly dismissed, but readily gained. *["I never used to pay much attention to what was being said around me or to me, I was too busy worrying about the graded part of an activity, comparing myself and how I did to others. But now I have learned to let what I read and hear take on meaning for me."— Jennie (twelfth grade)]*

Journal Entry: Perhaps I should forget everything I think I know about methods and practices and ideas and ways to bring students to the technicalities of reading and writing. I don't want to forget that words have an innate voice that speaks strong and clear when we remember how to listen to the message. There is power in the creative force.

"All we can do," says Maxine Greene, "is cultivate multiple ways of seeing and multiple dialogues in a world where nothing stays the same" (1995, 16). Schools, however, are notorious for believing that a systematic approach to learning is the most effective and sensible. Like Plato, who lashed out at the poets of his day in suspicion that the "wrong" good might be actualized, schools superimpose hierarchical traditions of thought and action on teachers in hopes of controlling what students learn. But in communities bursting with a multitude of story lines, these traditions become nothing more than impediments, working only (and even then minimally) for those who can relate or reform. Though this may not be the intent of those who propose such an approach, it is the impression many students get and the one many teachers feel forced to work from, even when it clearly fails. There is little room for students to reveal who they are and even less opportunity for creating who they may want to be. Rather than being viewed as a place where important things happen, school becomes known as a sterile and stagnant site invented for the interests of those who run it and not those who attend it.

From the time we are old enough to understand there is an expected way of being in the world, the majority of us accept and internalize the codes and systems that prevail. They infiltrate most aspects of our lives, including how we do our work and how we perceive the actions and attentions of others within our organized communities. Though there is no doubt that much of what these organized systems of living do is make it possible to live sane and relatively safe lives, it remains imperative that we question the habitual roots of our practices lest we become so accustomed to them that we assume them as fixed truths. It is only when we examine other ways of knowing the world that we come to more meaningful recognitions about the life we share. *("Learning? certainly, but living primarily, and learning through and in relation to this living."* [Dewey 1899/1976, 25]) As teachers, it may even be seen as our duty to do so.

Lately, I have had reason to sift through belongings, mementos, pictures, and papers accumulated over the course of years. It did not take long for the diverse relics of my teaching career to surface. Looking around, I note they are everywhere. Here is a picture of Jerome, who went on to get a master's degree. *(This is my mom, he used to tell people. We would both laugh at their baffled response, for Jerome is black and I am white. His real mom was addicted to crack and died too young.)* Here is a pile of "thank you" notes, one from Dwain, another from Anne, and a hard-earned one from Dee-Dee and Shewan. "Thank you," they say. "Thank you." "Thank YOU," I whisper back to them. "Thank YOU." *(You especially, Shewan. You who taught me how one can be grateful even through the worst, the very worst of things. You especially, I thank.)* There is a night light from Russia brought back by Michael the year he made the "peace child" program and a clock in the shape of Virginia made special for me by Yolanda and her dad the year she graduated. A little harlequin mirror hangs on the wall, a t-shirt signed by a whole class of students is at the bottom of a drawer, and a pin crafted carefully from a collection of old buttons peers out from my jewelry box. Donald's mother made me the pin. "For believing in Donald," she said when she handed it to me. It is a fine pin, a keeper. Among the jewelry I find a silver charm that catches me off-guard. A picture flashes through my mind of the kids who presented it to me. On one side of the piece is the mask of comedy, on the other, tragedy. I spin it on its chain and in the spinning cannot tell the two sides apart. It is a gem of a find, a fitting and eloquent treasure. I can bring myself to throw nothing away. *(Give, I remind myself, but know too how to receive.)*

How do we tell someone the stories of our days as teachers, days so rich in sorrow and delight? How do we express the daily sharing in the lives of our students that augments our own, fills us to overflowing, makes us emotionally fat? *(Ms. O'Quinn: I think this is a great class. Sometimes after I leave I want to come back.—Lavi)* How do we benchmark or measure the value of a day made successful by the gain of another's trust or failed because of someone's human frailty (often our own)? How do we, quoting Wm. Carlos Wms., keep our "craft" [from] becoming "subverted by thought"? Though Williams spoke with moral concern for his writing, educators must ask of their own professional lives the same piercing question.

Journal Entry: I've been talking to the kids about *Li'l Abner*. They're a bit leery, but interested. They love that we might use real animals for the "Dogpatch, USA" number. Jerri says we can get a piglet from her dad's farm. Donnie can bring in some caged chickens. Kathy has twin dalmations that might look pretty cool (already I imagine someone in a polka-dot dress on stage with those two dogs), and Mark said his aunt has a pet groundhog that would probably behave long enough to get through the scene! My God, a pet groundhog. Who are my students? What richnesses of life have I missed that they not only enjoy but rejoice in?

Floundering with Grace

It is early in my career as an English teacher, and I am standing in front of my class reading aloud from Walt Whitman. I am eager and animated. As we come to the end of the poem, my students are stunned by what I am reading. It is heresy. I remember the exact passage. It is the final lines from "Song of Myself":

> "Writing and talk do not prove me,
> I carry the plenum of proof and every thing else in my face,
> With the hush of my lips I wholly confound the skeptic."

We have been discussing the poem up to this point, so the students are well aware of the message implied by these words. As I finish reading, I close the book, look at them, and ask, "So, what do you think?" Nothing. I recite the three lines again. Walking down the aisles, swooshing my arms through the air, hitting my fist on a desk, I repeat, "Writing and talk do not prove me...." I wait. Larry, who I have noticed is out of school more than he is in, says in a brazen voice, "No one cares how we really are, only what they think they can teach us to be. Who we really are doesn't matter." I am bolted into silence. I have discovered pretty quickly the underlying truth of his words, but this is the first time that truth has been articulated. The voices of my students have been stilled in direct irony to the point Walt tries to make. We pause and look again at the poet's words; this time I ask them to look through the lens of their lives.

One of the earliest lessons I learned about teaching was that I, too, was expected to abide by a formulated definition of who to be in school. *("No one cares how we really are...")* As teachers, we may not give as much thought as we should to the subtle conflicts awaiting us in school, conflicts brought on by what can be major philosophical differences in determining curricular needs, experimenting with pedagogical practice, and encouraging growth. Most of us uncover these dissimilarities only gradually. In fact, before teaching, I never thought in any extended personal sense about issues of power and authority in schools and recognized even less how such issues have the capacity to undermine the strengths of teachers as much as students. Larry's exclamation was my first true testimony to the fact of this insight. Like the students, I generally ignored the bureaucracy that came my way, accepting, for the most part, that some things were "just like that."

However, it did not take me long to see that the idea of power through expectation was the big stick used to measure progress in schools, mine as well as that of my students. It was one of the "unspoken" tenets of teaching that often made my daily work feel like I was under house arrest. My classes could move (as could I), but only within a restricted arena. Initially, I was just flat out overwhelmed by this discovery. I could not figure out how to preserve the elements of wonder I felt conducive to a progressive learning environment while appeasing the many demands of the bureaucratic system of which I was a part. Moreso, I could not believe the toll that such thinking was taking on my ability to unleash the creative dynamics of the classroom community. For months I walked around amazed at the differences between what I had anticipated my classroom would be, what I was being asked to make it, and what, from their experiences, the students were expecting from it. I felt it was assumed I would disown not only in my students but also in myself all but the most superficial principles of self-expression. It was a confusing, distressing, and horribly alien feeling. Students rarely questioned, knew better how to respond than reflect, and almost totally separated the culture of self from the culture of learning. Still, I knew I had a duty to do better by us all.

And so I learned to bring in readings, personal writings, and ideas from the world outside of the class and had the students do the same. We interspersed those things with choices made from the text and suggestions explicit in the curriculum. I also learned to keep the classroom door closed, not to keep something out, but to ensure that learning might expand from within. When our time together was over, I wanted to be sure we had all grown in our understanding not only of English, but also in our understanding of what it means to be human. I wanted students to know that our intrinsic worth might be groomed through correction, but was formed by a recognition of personal vulnerability and public compassion. *[Ms. O'Quinn, I've learned that if you actually listen to what a person is saying, instead of just hearing the words, you can get a message—Marie (Tenth grade)].* Though we might lose some of our innocence in the search for a literacy experience *(In innocence we grow wise. Paradox is embraced, not ignored.),* at least we might also find the heart necessary for a broadened vision of what it means to be educated.

Journal Entry: As teachers we can't go about the business of schooling minds while ignoring the education of the fragile nature of bodies and souls. To do so is to perpetuate a society of people who know much about process and product and little about acceptance and fulfillment; who recognize readily the failings of others while falling constantly short in their own potential; who live protected by conscience while understanding nothing about consciousness.

What *if* I had understood from the first day of entering a classroom that good teaching is as much about the search for wisdom as it is the search for knowledge? Would I have seen more of the promise of my students, imposed less of myself, and had more small moments of insight? Would things have been different if I knew to wait in patient silence for the ordinariness of things to reveal themselves?

What *if* I had been told as a new teacher to set aside my fears of failure in order that I could attend more clearly to the threat my students felt about their own perceived inadequacies? Would I have been more generous with the weak, more gentle with the strong? Might I have learned sooner not to eclipse the faint shine of my more apprehensive students or bully back the brawn of the most robust?

What *if* I had learned sooner to push my students to explore possibilities rather than seek after truths? Would they have been better able to hear not only their own stories but the stories of others as well? Would learning have been more a momentous adventure and less a monotonous task had I known enough to believe as much in my students as I did in what I thought I had learned in school?

(What if I had known? Would a student's life be different? Would my own?)

Going Forth Daily

It is late on a summer night, and I am lying in bed listening to the sounds of the neighborhood. In a slow swirl, the fan above me surrounds my bed with a sweep of warm fragrant air. The phone rings. It is Katina, calling from the dorm of a residential, academic summer program she is in. I direct the program. Her mother is drunk, on the front lawn, raising hell, scaring the rest of the girls, yelling she wants Katina to come home. The child is terrified, crying. She does not want to go. I tell her to sit tight, I will be right there, and then I call campus safety to go over to the dorm and get the mother off the grounds.

By the time I get there, the mother has left but is on the phone, asking to speak to me. She tells me I can have her daughter (She is not the only person to tell me I can have their child.); she is sick of her; and I am a witch for interfering with their life. (The reference is to the calls I have made to Katina's siblings seeking their help.) I take Katina home with me that night and give her a place in the guest room. She cries most of the night. (My colleagues give me a hard time about bringing a child home. I could get in big trouble. *Risk, I remind myself. Courage. Lots of it.*) Katina keeps saying she cannot believe I would bring her home. She is crying just as much over that as anything. It is apparent she is unaccustomed to kindness. I let her stay a few nights while I continue to call and try to convince her older sister to please help. It is to no avail.

When I feel that Katina is out of immediate danger, I let her go back to sleeping at the dorm. The mother acts as if nothing ever happened, thanks me for taking such an interest in "the girl." Before she leaves my house, I give Katina a stuffed doll she admires from the bed in the guest room. I tell her to find comfort in it whenever things are looking impossible, that it will not be long until she can more easily realize the possibilities of her own life. Later she tells me she keeps it with her the whole time she is in college, a reminder of what she must do not only for herself, but also for others in similar situations.

I am changed by the experience with Katina in a place deep within me. As I write these words, I ache all over again for her and the thousands of students like her who I know fill our classrooms every day; but I am strengthened too in knowing that despite all that happened, Katina reached her dream of finishing college and becoming a social worker. It was a rough four years, but she made it. Till this day, I keep in my treasure trove of school things her graduation announcement. It is evidence to me of what happens when students learn to believe in themselves, know others believe in them, and take incredible risks despite circumstances that regularly seem insurmountable. I am proud of Katina. I feel lucky and humbled to have known her.

I once told a group of people that I became a teacher because I could not be a gypsy, and though my comment in part was jest, in retrospect I see some underlying truths to it. In regular exchange and engagement with strangers, I learn to respect the fragilities and strengths of my own character. I learn that what others think and how I interact with their thinking brings great bearing on the community we build together. Teaching has always been an intense and affirming love affair between my students and me, one held together with tremendous promise and possibility and dependent in part on duty and honor and in part on the awe and wonder of it all. As is the case in all great loves, there is enormous risk in the trusting of the heart and the baring of the soul, yet through that risk we are able as both teacher and student to once again value and believe in the goodness of ourselves and our dreams.

It is important to recognize that the pleasure and worth in what a teacher does comes not much at all from the actual imparting of fact and figure. It flourishes instead from the shared wealth of lives that connect, embrace, and reverberate each to the other. It calls wisdom to the forefront and, despite the tension, respects ongoing struggles with uncertainty. The teacher, regardless of what the conventional mindset would have us believe, does not live in a world composed of industry and project. The organic nature of the classroom does not allow for that. To envision it as such is to relegate it to the doldrums of authoritative habit rather than the grace of the greater good. Reverent teachers see beyond tiresome endings. Like the legendary phoenix, they rise again and again into the sky, certain of the boundless landscape and the sound of rushing air that whispers infinite in hope and in ever new beginnings.

Journal Entry: I heard today that Jack is retiring from teaching. He's given his life to it. Though he jokingly talked about days on the golf course, he also said he doesn't know what to think about a day without students. They're his lifeblood. I tried to be jovial with him, suggesting he won't miss the kids for long, that looking at all that bad writing will certainly not be missed, and that, finally, he may have time for his own dust-covered projects. It didn't help much. I could tell a piece of him will stay behind. Jack's passion has always been his students. What moves him is the meaning they share and create; cursing them, crying with them, laughing with them has been his life. Reading a passage of poetry over and over again until the raw emotion of it is new life breathed into everyone is Jack's labor of love. Pushing for

ideas and ideals and recognizing the worst right up next to the best has been his pursuit. Jack has given his students what no book, theory, or philosophy, or school of thought, or rule, or principle, or standard could ever provide. He's opened his heart and given freely and generously of everything that therein lies. He's made the private public. He's taken risks and covered dangerous ground. He's cared and dreamed and expected as much for his students as he has for himself. If a camera could capture the picture, the lines where Jack ends and his students begin would be indistinguishable. For he's learned well the lesson that Whitman acclaims: "I and mine do not convince by arguments, similes, rhymes. We convince by our presence." Jack has revered his students and his profession. I am humbled forever in this knowledge.

(Only with wakeful eye can we see the promise of that which might be and the telling passion of that which is. In quiet recognition of all that is yet to come, teachers move boldly, indivisibly forward. With each step, the whole of the world is revealed, each experience forever treasured).

References

Dewey, J. 1899/1976. *The School and Society*. In *John Dewey: The Middle Works*, Volume 1. Edited by Jo Ann Boydston, 1–109. Carbondale: Southern Illinois University Press.

Emerson, R. 1957. *Selections from Ralph Waldo Emerson*. Edited by Stephen Whicher. Boston: Houghton Mifflin.

Fine, M. 1992. *Disruptive Voices: The Possibilities of Feminist Research*. Ann Arbor: University of Michigan Press.

Gluck, L. 1993. *The Wild Iris*. Hopewell, NJ: Ecco Press.

Greene, M. 1995. *Releasing the Imagination: Essays on Education, the Arts, and Social Change*. San Francisco: Jossey-Bass.

Johnson, M. 1993. *Moral Imagination: Implications of Cognitive Science for Ethics*. Chicago: University of Chicago Press.

Stevens, W. 1990. *Wallace Stevens: The Collected Poems*. New York: Random House.

Whitman, W. 1959. *Complete Poetry and Selected Prose*. Edited by James E. Miller Jr. Boston: Houghton Mifflin.

7

Reverence for What? A Teacher's Quest

William H. Schubert

Reverence has had many meanings for me as I have journeyed over six decades in this curriculum called my life. I want to share some of them here in hopes that readers will reconstruct and reflect on the meanings of reverence that have brought them to their own current juncture. Thus, to illustrate, I begin by recalling my childhood, youth, academic life, young adulthood, elementary teaching experience, and continue with my life as a professor. I note strengths and limitations of the succession of objects of my sense of reverence along the way. Without giving away the ending, as children often say in their book reports, I conclude by sketching where this journey puts me today. As for a hint about this, I have felt as edified by the quest as by any of the objects of reverence that captivated me at a given time. So, now into the story.

Reverence in Sanctioned Authority

Reverend Schubert: that is what my maternal grandmother and her twin sister respectfully called my father's father. He was a Lutheran minister of the Missouri Synod variety—now deemed highly conservative. I don't know if there was another variety in 1903, when he arrived in Springfield, Illinois, to attend seminary at age eighteen—emigrating all the way from Jonsdorf, Germany. I knew him as Grandpa Schubert, a retired minister whom I saw in the pulpit in Berea, Ohio (a suburb of Cleveland), a couple of times, and heard many refer to him as *Reverend*. At age five or six, I could readily tell that he was attributed with special respect. So, I was not surprised with the response of my parents to one of my first philosophical questions: "Who came first; Adam and Eve or the cave men?" My parents said that I should wait until the next time Grandpa Schubert came to our small town in northeast Indiana for his next visit. They said he was an expert in answering such questions. He traveled to our rural community a couple of times each year, and my parents probably thought, or perhaps hoped, that I might forget to ask him. Nevertheless, when he arrived several months hence, I ran to his car ignoring the gifts of candy he often brought, and asked, "Who came first—Adam and Eve or the cave men?" His startled response was, "Some think Adam and Eve and some think the cave men." That was the discussion. I was taken aback. I wondered what *expertise* meant. Though I could not express it as such, I wondered what *Reverend* and *reverence* signify.

Surely, this incident signifies a beginning of my educational quest—a phenomenon of my life in over forty years of teaching. This experience has taught me that unless there is a sense of awe for something, something mysterious or too pervasive to understand, pursuit of understanding is weakened. My quest to know and to grow, and to share thereof, thus to teach, can be seen as a continuous search for spheres of awe and sources of reverence. I moved through several of these during several phases of my life, and I continue to do so.

As portrayed vividly by Paul Woodruff (2001), reverence is a neglected virtue embedded in our being from the earliest inklings of culture, ceremony, and other attempts to gather the meaning of life—expressed in awe for what is deemed greater than oneself. While reverence has found expression in religions, as illustrated with my grandfather, it is not solely or even primarily to be associated with extant religions. It is about the centrality of human pondering of the profound, the infinite, the filial, the inexpressible, the venerable, the commendable, that which is worth honoring. So, what has been worth honoring in my life? How has it cultivated my interest in becoming more fully educated? How has it elicited my desire to share with others—to teach? I offer stories and observations about these matters, episodes of my life, because I hope they evoke reflection on the place of reverence in the lives of others—a hope couched in the assumption of *a common faith* (Dewey 1934) that together we will strive toward the highest human potential.

Stories of awe-inspiring pasts are both discarded and remain. I have revered certain forces in life, discarded them, knowing full well that their imprint remains within me in ways that I can barely detect. Seeking reverence, something worth revering, in several passages of my life I have questioned the meaning of trust I should attribute for that which is worth the label *reverend*. So, when as a child, I remained confused about whether

Adam and Eve came before or after cave dwellers, the idea of appeal to authority doubtless remained encoded in my educational pursuits. What took its place?

Reverence in Cultural Constructs: Basketball and Fundamentalist Religion

I was bouncing a balloon near the stairway of our house at about age seven—announcing the game. What game? The one I made up, while my parents listened to the radio broadcast of one of the most salient events in Hoosier life—the Indiana High School Basketball Tournament—*Hoosier hysteria*. My version of the game was to imagine a nine-foot-tall player named Jim and a twelve-foot-tall player named (naturally) Bill, who no opponent could stop, and to announce (mimicking the play-by-play description I heard on the radio) how Jim passed the ball(oon) to Bill who easily put the ball *down* into the basket. At that moment, I joined the vast majority of the Hoosier state in revering basketball prowess as the quintessence of personal achievement—an accomplishment worth all of the awe and reverence one could extend. Pillars of the community were judged on the basis of shots made or missed as adolescents more than on their career accomplishments thirty or forty years after their days as teenage roundball shooting knights who defended their community's reputation against that of nearby towns. Dad was a coach of all sports (also superintendent, principal, shop teacher, and commercial teacher) for a school so small that it had no town and only about twenty boys from which to select a high school basketball team. Nonetheless, in 1952, he took them to the Sectional Tournament finals against a team that recently made the Indiana final four—the movie *Hoosiers* in microcosm! Three players from his school got basketball scholarships to small colleges. They were my heroes. Ten years later the team on which I played made it to the championship of that same sectional. In the decade between the two championship games, my imagination soared in creation of a fictional basketball team that I called Bakersville. I conjured up high school players who rivaled the then dominant Boston Celtics of the National Basketball Association. Pat Rolleum, superstar of Bakersville, was ensconced in my psyche so deeply that, forty years later, after I gave a lecture to school administrators in the 1990s in Springfield, Massachusetts, I was compelled to write a tribute to him and stealthily install him in a display at the Basketball Hall of Fame (for which I may be forbidden admission after this chapter is read by the basketball guardians). To me, and to many others in the Golden Years of Indiana high school basketball (circa 1940s through 1970s), basketball was more than a sport, it was a pinnacle of life. Should it have been? Good question. Nevertheless, there is a book called *Hoosier Temples*, commentaries on and photographs of unique local gymnasiums, the construction of which was an expression of reverence to the home team. Moreover, this small state sports nineteen of the twenty largest high school gyms in the United States, and the seating capacity of several exceeds the population of the towns that built them, and capacity crowds always filled them. Additional tickets were not available! Reverence? Little question. Should reverence have been accorded? Considerable question. I was too immersed, at the time to address this question however.

In small-town Indiana, indicative of small-town America, another great force reigned strong: fundamentalist Christianity. Most of my peers, including the most successful students in my class, were fundamentalist. My family belonged to the country club church—the one that catered to the business and professional group in town—the only one (of many) that was not fundamentalist. At the time, the fundamentalist kids seemed sincerely to try to live their creed. I tried to be one of them. They told me that no one should be called Reverend but (of course) Jesus. That made me recall Grandpa Schubert, who was by then deceased. I sadly pondered that rule. The fundamentalists thought the best book, the only really meaningful book, was the Bible. I took this point seriously enough that I convinced the English teacher that she should count books of the Bible (some of which are only a few pages in length) as sufficient for extra required book reports or she did not believe fully in the Bible. She reluctantly accepted my proposal, probably due to perceived pressure from the social milieu of a largely fundamentalist community, if she did not and if it was made known. With my good friends, as teens are wont to do, we discussed the meaning of life and our purpose in it—almost always, however, from a fundamentalist perspective.

Reverence for the Liberal Arts and *Great Ideas*

I became one of the very few from my community to go to college—albeit a small liberal arts college that was church related, though not fundamentalist. Although I had been exposed to a range of literature and ideas in school and from my family, who were college educated, peer domination had prevented me from taking it seriously as a source of figuring out who I was and what I might strive to become—keeping basketball and fundamentalism as my sources of reverence. In college, however, I found a new sense of awe, a source of reverence unaccepted by me before: a liberal education. In pondering literature, philosophy, sciences, and arts, I found deeper sources of meaning. I recall the moment reading literary criticism in the college library that I thought, "This is about what I've talked about with my friends at our deepest moments—though it is deeper and embedded in the characters, events, and discussions of a liberal education. Of course, it was still a largely Western liberal education—though so much richer than my reliance on authority of labels such as Rev., or militaristic emulations such as basketball, or true believers such as fundamentalists. Still, I kept a skeptical respect for those with labeled credentials as possibly knowledgeable, arbitrary rules of games as societal glue, and associations of like-minded strivers for goodness as exemplars of worthy attempt.

It was the newly found liberal education that propelled me into a state of reverence for the sages of today and yesteryear—those who I wanted to stand with—apart from the exigencies of worldly affliction that seemed to pale before the greatest insight of the ages. It was then that I became committed to teach. I came from a family of teachers: Mom, Dad, Grandma, two great aunts, a great grandfather, and grandfather who taught through the ministry and another who taught as a farmer-politician. In teenage rebellion, I had temporarily departed from this familial legacy; however, and at age nineteen decided I wanted to commit my career to showing children and youths that there was a larger more awesome source of meaning than they might find in the daily experience of their neighborhoods and communities. I wanted to offer a kind of education that enabled them to compose their lives (though it would be over two decades until Mary Catherine Bateson, 1989, would write a book based on this image).

Reverence for Progressive Theory and Practice

While I became credentialed to be an elementary school teacher through my undergraduate studies, I wanted to study philosophy, literature, and educational philosophy and history more fully, so I did so during the remainder of my undergraduate studies. Then, I pursued a master's degree with noted Deweyan philosophers (A. Stafford Clayton, Stanley E. Ballinger, Malcolm Skilbeck, and Philip G. Smith) at Indiana University. Along with the culture shock of moving in the early 1960s, during civil rights and antiwar movements, from Manchester (a pacifist college) to the world of Indiana University at Bloomington, where to be anti-administration was far from being antiwar instead of prowar at Manchester, I found philosophical orientations that challenged my reverence for traditional liberal education. A whole course, by Professor Clayton, fashioned around Dewey's *Democracy and Education* (1916) helped me revere education as a function of individual and collective interest engaged in endless democratic struggle and enactment. I discovered that curriculum development literature grew from such considerations (e.g., Bruner 1960; Smith, Stanley, and Shores 1957), and I wondered why curriculum was equated in teacher preparation course work with uncritical, unproblematized lesson or unit planning. I studied a range of philosophical orientations that I missed in undergraduate school, including personality theorists derived from the early psychoanalytic traditions. When encouraged to start doctoral work, I felt too inexperienced, and knew I needed to teach in public schools if ever I was to help teachers become public educators. I needed to test my conflicting theoretical commitments in the crucible of practice. Though I was too irreverent to say so at the time, I may have sensed a need to discover my next source of reverence through the practice of teaching.

Reverence for Student Interests

As an elementary school teacher in a suburban Chicago district with a reputation for progressive theory and practice, I still had to struggle to engage students in the creation of their educational experience as an effort to consciously compose their lives. I quickly concluded that in becoming a better teacher one could not rely on professional development sessions offered by the school, despite the fact that some were inspiring and informative. My personally designed professional development consisted of reading philosophy and literature, experiencing the arts community of the Chicago area, and engaging in philosophical discourse with revered colleagues, friends, and relatives. Increasingly, I began to recognize some of these colleagues as my students themselves, even though they were in the age range of nine to twelve.

What I discovered during my eight-year sojourn in elementary school teaching was that the liberal arts can be liberating at the deepest level of Deweyan progressive pedagogical praxis. Colleague teachers often lamented that they would like to use a Deweyan approach but could not do so because of the numbers of students. They said that they could not make a separate curriculum for each of the thirty students. High school teachers were even more animated in this caveat, seeing more than 125 students each day. I often taught using *interest groups*, in which I asked students to identify an interest they were never before permitted to pursue in school. At first, this seemed impossible, given the fifty-five–sixty-five students for whom I was responsible in an open space, differentiated staffing educational environment. Nonetheless, what I discovered as I let the situation grow was that conversation would connect initially separate interests, and as they moved along, individual interests were transformed into communal interests—basic human interests (Habermas 1971) or what Robert Ulich insightfully called the "great events and mysteries of life: birth, death, love, tradition, society and the crowd, success and failure, salvation, and anxiety" (1955, 255). These, of course, are illustrative, not exhaustive. Initial interests involved a great deal of popular culture—peer interests, sports, clubs, after school lessons, church, television, movies, pop music, many other forms of media, family relations, food, cultural mores and folkways, overcoming restrictions, and much more. All of these are sources they used to make meaning of their lives, interpret their pasts, imagine and plan their possibilities.

At their core, these interests bespeak essences of a liberal education that are liberating—reasons for studying, ways to compose their lives, dimensions of so-called great ideas that too often remain external to lived experience and reflection upon it. Playing with and teaching my own children also helped me perceive what I consider a natural human desire to probe deeply into who we are, who we want to become, and how we hope to go there. I clearly do not want to convey the impression that I was always successful in accomplishing this kind and quality of educational experience, in school or out of school. When I did catch a glimmer of success in this endeavor, however, it captured my desire to continue to be an educator. Reverence for this possibility was what I wanted to enable others to experience.

When I considered pursuing a Ph.D., I pondered what I had discovered in my teaching career. I decided to design a dissertation that communicated something of the essence of this, by highlighting what I considered to be the two main tools of my teaching, imagination and philosophy, neither of which is a commodity to be bought or sold. Simultaneously, as a graduate teaching assistant, I began teaching undergraduates who were preparing to be elementary teachers, so I tried to communicate my central learning about teaching to them. Their responses became integrated in my dissertation, as did explorations in literature, philosophy, and the history of progressive education. So did the experientially based advice of educators I revered. J. Harlan Shores, my advisor, encouraged me to look far and wide in theory and practice for relationships between philosophy and imagination, enhancing a teacher's capacity to anticipate. I asked my father, too, what he gleaned from nearly forty years of being a teacher, coach, and school administrator to teach teachers. He said, rather surprisingly to me (given his long history of a no-nonsense but highly respected work) that teachers should know how to feel the hurt inside the child and they should learn to speak the language of the children. I renewed, on the spot, my respect for my father. My mother, too, exemplified traits as a teacher that brought her students to rate her as their favorite high school teacher on several occasions and to give her a standing ovation at a class reunion twenty-five years later.

Reverence for Close Relationships

I thought, too, about my closest relationships (friends and loved ones) over past years and at present (friends and loved ones) and how they influenced my teaching through both commonality and expansion. Coming to know kindred spirits with common interests brought connection or convergence, while expansiveness opened new doors of divergence. I may have revered relationships that brought both convergence and divergence. For a while I thought that it should; however, I have recently wondered if there is not something deeper that should be revered. Relationships that simultaneously bring convergence and divergence strike me as being living instantiations of Vygotsky's (1962) zone of proximal development, the basis of readiness to learn the novel (divergence) when it is connected with understandings deeply held (convergence).

Beyond Objects of Reverence

I pondered all of the above. I thought again of my transformations of reverence and the discarded, though still lingering, objects revered. As a young child, I wanted to believe in reverence for authority to know if Adam and Eve preceded cave dwellers, and rejected authority because it announced uncertainty. Later, immersed in a culture that worshiped basketball, I sought a basis for reverence in recognition of performance on the courts, only to later recognize the game as an arbitrary construct. Also, as a teenager, I searched for sources of reverence in the fundamentalist Christian subculture that surrounded me, ultimately feeling deluded. The intellectual milieu of a liberal arts college taught me to revere the great minds and ideas that flowed from them, although that became stale and brittle in the countenance of public knowledge and ideological criticism.

As I encountered John Dewey's progressive attention to interests in lived experience and tried to be an elementary school teacher (and later professor of education) within a progressive ethos, I implicitly wondered if I should be reverent of something in that realm of experience. I doubted, however, if it made sense to revere the entire panoply of interests hewn from experience. I worried that if I revered everything, then I slipped into a state of pervasive reverence for nothing. Alternatively, if I blatantly stated that I had reverence for nothing, I could not live with the arrogance: reverence for the irreverent. Although I wondered if it was really arrogance, or if it was merely an existential continuation of the conclusion that in an absurd world, wherein we need to construct purpose to have reason for being. By accepting such construction, I wondered if any revered object or idea becomes a kind of fiction. So, I entertained whether I should revere fiction. I wondered if I should or could give up a desire to experience genuine awe, because such a quest is a will-o'-the-wisp.

I often turned to stories, novels, and plays for solace in this predicament. But I cannot say that I revered them. Similarly, I wondered if I should say that I had reverence for relationships—even the best relationships I encountered. Relationships are not permanent—they vacillate and change, but it seems too vague, too intangible, to revere mere change. Still, I don't want to get into a reincarnated debate between whether all is change (Heraclitus) or all is permanence (Parmenides). Clearly, something does not have to be verified as permanent in order to be revered. So what did I revere? I was immobilized.

I stopped writing the draft of this chapter in May and resumed in September. In the interim I traveled to China, Vancouver, Florida, Georgia, North and South Carolina, Kentucky and Tennessee, Ohio, Indiana, and Illinois. Granted, I was not on a pilgrimage to find reverence; however, I did ponder it. In China, for instance, I felt close to the Taoist tradition submerged in natural beauty of the forests, fields, and exquisite gardens, though I can only skirt the magnitude of its depth. Yet, in such settings I could simply turn in a nearby direction and be pierced by myriad stores and products that bespeak Westernized globalization. Still, despite the jarring of these incongruities, the holistic connection among humans and nature made me ponder the possibility of reverence for connection, for wholeness. Also, in the majestic surrounds of Vancouver—the sea, the lakes, the snow-capped peaks, and the invigorating fresh air, I felt immersed in wholeness—as I had felt in a Buddhist temple in Changzhou, or while floating across the Yangtze River, and as I was admiring the canal adorned gardens of Suzhou. Walking in the surf and sands of Florida's east coast reminded me of the awe of my first visit to the Atlantic at age eight, when I speculated that if I just had powerful enough vision, I could see Africa and Europe. Other memories erupted as I stood among the giant entwined oak trees on Jekyll Island, off the coast of Georgia, and thought of my tree-climbing escapades with Jerry, my childhood buddy, as we pretended to be monkeys eating weeping willow leaf bananas. Closeness to trees, by the way, prompted me (as an elementary school teacher) to ask each sixth grader in outdoor education sojourns in the Wisconsin woods to get to know a tree, talk to it of its historical experience, and then introduce that tree to classmates.

Reverence for Teacher Learning

As I moved from elementary school teaching into the educational professoriate, I asked myself what I had learned from my studies, as well as from my teaching, to share with educators at the undergraduate and graduate levels. At first, I came to the same answer as when I had asked a similar question after completing six years of elementary school teaching and moving into the sabbatical leave wherein I completed the course work for my Ph.D. Wanting to complete the Ph.D. as efficiently (effectively, too, of course) as possible, I determined that philosophy and imagination were the major tools I wanted to convey to prospective teachers. I turned all of my Ph.D. coursework and reading into a quest to understand more about the role of both in teaching and curriculum. This resulted in a dissertation that explored what I called *imaginative projection*, which I saw as a method of curriculum invention in the process of teaching (Schubert 1975). As we teach, I argued, we continuously refine our philosophy through reflection on experience and through study, and we simultaneously hone our imagination as we live our philosophy in the experiences (curricula) of teaching and learning situations. I drew upon multiple research orientations to understand and express this perspective: historical inquiry into progressive education; literary sources on imagination; study of selected philosophical classics; interpretative analyses of my own teaching; a dialogic narrative study of several classroom teachers from the bizarre standpoint (a fictionalized pair of intergalactic educational anthropologists discussing an article on education of Earthlings for an *Intergalactic Encyclopedia of Educational Research*); strategies for teachers to develop their imaginative and reflective capacities; a quasi-experimental comparative (experimental and control group comparison) study of those who were taught the strategies I developed and those who were not; qualitative follow-up interviews of the participants; and a participant-observer study of imaginative projection in my own practice as an elementary school teacher, after I returned to teaching to repay the sabbatical leave.

Reverence for "What Is Worthwhile?"

After completing the dissertation, as I said, I again asked myself what I deemed worthwhile to teach teachers. I began to answer this question in a similar manner as I did prior to doctoral studies—developing philosophical and imaginative capacities. I was conflicted, however. What kind of philosophy and what view of imagination should guide me? I knew that I wanted to enable educators to ponder their educational life reflectively, but

I was perplexed by HOW. In my work with those who wanted to be teachers or educational leaders and eventually those who wanted to be curriculum scholars and professors, I was committed to building communities of scholar-practitioners or scholar-professors. But for what? I wanted to share with them ideas and feelings that inspired previous generations of educators, and was convinced that doing so had to centrally embrace what I considered the basic curriculum question. In some legitimate way, they needed to address the basic curriculum question: What is worthwhile? As I gained experience and studied more, I wanted to wonder with my colleagues and students: What is worth knowing, needing, experiencing, doing, being, becoming, overcoming, sharing, contributing, and wondering (Schubert 2009b)? Moreover, I saw the addressing of such questions as a process of building a life—returning to the image Bateson (1989) has called *composing a life*. Today, I contend that building a life is the most important educational project human beings have. In order to build lives they must ask questions about what is worthwhile, such as those noted above (Schubert 2009b). Living a worthwhile life is surely not a solitary matter. It involves the contributions of that life in the world; thus, it must be public and political as well as personal (Ayers 2004).

Reverence for the Quest

If we are to act with reverence to something, then, it is the process of seeking that which is worthwhile in our lives and in the world. This, I contend, supersedes the authority of experts, cultural ceremonies, gods, states, particular relationships, or even nature. It is reverence for the process of seeking, for sharing that process with others, for appreciating it when we see it in lived experience, and for realizing that answers about what is worthwhile are at best situational, submerged in the flow of lived experience, and always tentative within the changing currents of that flow (see He 2003). Possibilities are continually elusive and worth exploring.

This posture on reverence did not come to me a priori; rather, it evolved a posteriori, during forty-three years as an educator—eight with elementary school students and thirty-five with undergraduate and graduate students. In retrospect, I think I created group process strategies in my classes based on the best discussions I have had in informal settings with persons I knew well and cared about—individuals with whom I explored and continue to explore the meanings of life and possibilities for making worthwhile contributions. Such persons have not only been those with whom I have agreed. Rather, they often challenged my perspectives and ways of life. Such persons have pushed me to a state of being *in-between*, a philosophical state analogous to the cultural *in-between-ness* that Ming Fang He (2003) illuminates so poignantly in regard to the lives of women who were born in China and immigrated to Canada. Later, He's (2010) work elaborates being *in-between* to an *exile pedagogy*. I contend that one can be exiled from ideas that dominate their philosophy as well as from cultures because ideas embody a cultural milieu; exile can enhance imagination—liberating one from the chains of nationalism, orthodoxy, political or economic myopia, and monoculturalism, as well as from physical or emotional oppression. As a teacher I implicitly, if not explicitly, emulated these *teachers*—all fellow participants in dialogue—including myself as one of the *teachers*.

My emulation took many forms, one of which was a variation on a role-playing approach that I began doing as an elementary school teacher. I role-played those with whom I engaged in dialogue, as far-reaching as fictionalized prehistoric persons, other characters in history, proponents of propaganda used in advertising and elsewhere, advocates of pros and cons of studying different subject matter, characters in stories from literary sources, and much more (Schubert 1992). As a university faculty member, I felt as if I needed to expose students to diverse viewpoints, in a somewhat similar but developmentally appropriate manner for their needs. I wanted to build upon Theodore Brameld's (1956) productive notion of *defensible partiality* when working with controversial issues. He urged teachers or professors to give their own positions on a particular issue and then say that they would do their best to honestly portray different extant positions from that vantage point. However, given my propensity for role-playing, I languished more deeply in this dilemma of how to present positions. I was not sure where I stood on certain key issues. Moreover, I felt that deep within me lurked proponents of many conflicting issues. Some may see this as inconsistency or contradiction; however, I sided with Walt Whitman (1998/1855) on this one, when he says in his renowned *Song of Myself*:

> Do I contradict myself?
> Very well….then I contradict myself.
> I am large…. I contain multitudes.

Reverence for Engaging in the Quest with Students and Others

I decided to let the proponents of diverse viewpoints come forth in the form of *guest speakers*, as they came to be known. They took many forms; however, the *most frequent appearances award* goes, thus far, to four *guests*: the *intellectual traditionalist*, the *social behaviorist*, the *experientialist*, and the *critical reconstructionist*. While each of these disagrees, often feverishly, with the others, they are loosely bonded together by a common interest in the question of what is worthwhile, and when called upon, they fervently state their case. Moreover, each has helped me devise group process strategies that help students reflect on this central quest in considerably different ways (Schubert, 1996; 1997). Through the *guest speakers* I try to jog students to consider alternative views, to make them uncertain about their positions, and to encourage deeper and broader reflections. Such reflections to continuously reconstruct one's life is never finalized—always renewing, inquiring, acting, revisioning, reimagining, and overcoming. These *guests* or advocates visit my classes and work with students to expand their perspectives through reflection and discussion that reveal their own objects of reverence.

Observing and being part of students engaged in the process of bringing their objects of reverence to consciousness and attempting to articulate them is another object of reverence for me. When I see students struggle with their objects of reverence I see them in the throes of what powerful internal dialogue can be—education at a height of relevance. A few of the many examples: an African American man who tutored white classmates in a math class, helping them get grades of A or B and being given a D for the same work; a Pakistani woman whose concentration in class was clouded by floods experienced by family and friends in her homeland; a Chicago inner-city teacher who had already experienced four deaths in her high school; an award-winning art teacher who had lost her job due to budget cuts; a student who did not want progressive attention extended to her and wanted to remain anonymous because her previous teachers had treated her unfairly when they learned of her difficulties in life, thinking that she lacked potential. I am in awe of their capacity to overcome challenges in places I have not lived—places of class or gender, race or ethnicity, ability or disability, language or culture, place or Other-ness, danger or stressfulness, injustice or oppression. Their experience makes my own perspective become more robust. I am challenged by sources of reverence that have enabled them to deal with difficult times and make joyful times more fulfilling. In the face of such revelations, I see students identify and question sources of reverence and their desire to move to a more satisfying source, being unsatisfied even with that. I am in awe of resilience to *savage inequalities* (Kozol 1992) my students have experienced. I revere being part of their expressions of experience. This, of course, is not only the case with students. It pertains to the whole cast of characters that makes up my life (friends, relatives, colleagues, passersby), and I revere the ways in which it cultivates my sense of integrity, beauty, justice, and humanity—my being in the world.

Conclusion

A conclusion should always be a beginning. I have transitioned from seeking reverence in authority, cultural constructs such as basketball and fundamentalism, *great ideas* from liberal arts and sciences, progressive theory and practice, student interests, and close relationships. All of these can have considerable value, and they derive meaning from a deeper phenomenon, something that makes them meaningful—a more salient object of reverence—rather, a nonobject. For me, in this sixth decade of my life, I find that deeper phenomenon to be a continuous *quest* to seek what is worth knowing, needing, experiencing, doing, being, becoming, overcoming, sharing, contributing, and wondering. I try to illustrate this quest in a book based in John Dewey's sense of utopia (Schubert 2009a) wherein I search for meanings of and connections among love, justice, and education. Dewey (1933) clearly does not accept the conventional etymological derivation of utopia as perfection, rather as *search for* perfection in situations—recognizing that it is always illusive. Still, it is worth the search. Moreover, it is accentuated when I can participate in engaging students and others in the search. That is the heart of education as I see it—something clearly worth revering. Simply put, this teacher's search for reverence finds reverence for the search itself—continuous and always in flow.

References

Ayers, W. 2004. *Teaching the Personal and the Political: Essays on Hope and Justice*. New York: Teachers College Press.
Bateson, M. C. 1989. *Composing a Life*. New York: Atlantic Monthly Press.
Brameld, T. 1956. *Toward a Reconstructed Philosophy of Education*. New York: Holt, Rinehart, & Winston.
Bruner, J. 1960. *The Process of Education*. Cambridge, MA: Harvard University Press.
Dewey, J. 1916. *Democracy and Education*. New York: Macmillan.
———. 1933. Dewey outlines utopian schools. *New York Times*, April 23, E7.
———. 1934. *A Common Faith*. New Haven, CT: Yale University Press.
Habermas, J. 1971. *Knowledge and Human Interests*. Boston: Beacon.
He, M. F. 2003. *A River Forever Flowing: Cross-cultural Lives and Identities in the Multicultural Landscape*. Greenwich, CT: Information Age.
———. 2010. Exile Pedagogy: Teaching In-Between. In *Handbook of Public Pedagogy: Education and Learning beyond Schooling*, 469–482. Edited by J. A. Sandlin, B. D. Schultz, and J. Burdick. New York: Routledge.
Kozol, J. 1992. *Savage Inequalities: Children in America's Schools*. New York: Crown.

Schubert, W. H. 1975. *Imaginative Projection: A Method of Curriculum Invention.* Unpublished Ph.D. dissertation at the University of Illinois at Champaign-Urbana.

———. 1992. Our Journeys into Teaching: Remembering the Past. In *Teacher lore: Learning from Our Own Experiences*, 3–10. Edited by W. H. Schubert and W. Ayers. New York: Longman.

———. 1996. Perspectives on four curriculum traditions. *Educational Horizons* 74 (4): 169–176.

———. 1997. Character Education from Four Perspectives on Curriculum. In *The Construction of Children's Character*. NSSE Yearbook (Part II), 17–30. Edited by Alex Molnar. Chicago: University of Chicago Press and the National Society for the Study of Education.

———. 2009a. *Love, Justice, and Education: John Dewey and the Utopians.* Charlotte, NC: Information Age.

———. 2009b. What's worthwhile: From knowing and experiencing to being and becoming. *Journal of Curriculum and Pedagogy:* 21–39.

Smith, B. O., W. O., Stanley, and J. H. Shores. 1957. *Fundamentals of Curriculum Development.* New York: Harcourt, Brace, & World.

Ulich, R. 1955. Response to Ralph Harper's Essay. In *Modern Philosophies of Education, Fifty-Fourth Yearbook of the National Society for the Study of Education* (Part I), 254–257. Edited by N. B. Henry. Chicago: University of Chicago Press.

Vygotsky, L. S. 1962. *Thought and Language.* Cambridge, MA: MIT Press.

Whitman, W. 1998/1855. *Song of Myself.* Boston: Shambhala.

Woodruff, P. 2001. *Reverence: Renewing a Forgotten Virtue.* New York: Oxford University Press.

8

Lesson One: Reverence

William Ayers

My first lesson to those who teach and who think about becoming teachers would be to sing, as the Puerto Rican poet Judith Ortiz Cofer says in "Lesson One: I Would Sing," and I too use the hopeful conditional tense as she does (Cofer 1995, 60–63). The challenging work of teaching pivots on our ability to see the world as it is, without blinders or limits, and simultaneously to see our students as three-dimensional creatures—each a work-in-progress, each making her twisty way through a propulsive, uncertain history-in-the-making, each in this respect exactly like us. As they enter our classrooms we must reach out and recognize our students as full human beings with hopes and dreams, aspirations, skills, and capacities; with minds and hearts and spirits; with embodied experiences, histories, and stories to tell of a past and a possible future; with families, neighborhoods, cultural surrounds, and language communities all interacting, dynamic, and entangled. This knotty, complicated challenge is the intellectual and ethical heart of teaching, and it demands sustained focus, intelligent judgment, inquiry, and investigation. It calls forth within us an open heart and an inquiring mind and it reminds us that every one of our judgments is necessarily contingent, every view partial, and each conclusion tentative. It requires that we develop dispositions of patience, curiosity, respect, wonder, awe, and more than a small dose of humility—in short, a posture of reverence.

The challenge involves, then, an ethical stance and an implied moral contract. The good teacher offers unblinking recognition, and communicates a deep regard for students' lives, a respect for both their integrity and their vulnerability. An engaged teacher begins with a belief that each student is unique, each the one and only who will ever trod the earth, each worthy of a certain reverence. Regard extends, importantly, to the larger community—the wide, wide world that animates each individual life—since reverence for a specific person cannot be authentically expressed or realized while disparaging or despising the everything that brought forth that individual. Esteem includes insistence that students have access to the tools with which to negotiate and then to transform all that lies before them. Love for students just as they are—without any drive or advance toward a future—is false love, enervating and disabling. The teacher must try, in good faith, to do no harm, and then to convince students to reach out, to reinvent, and to seize an education fit for the fullest lives they might hope for. Another part of the work of teachers, then, is to see ourselves as in-transition, in-motion, works-in-progress.

Teaching in and for democracy is characterized by a spirit of cooperation, inclusion, social engagement, and full participation—classrooms become places that honor diversity while building unity. Democracy is based, after all, on the sense—at first intuited, and later more deliberate—that every human being is of incalculable value, that each is unique and distinct and still part of a wildly diverse whole, and that altogether we are, each and every one, somehow essential. We recognize, then, that the fullest development of all is the condition for the full development of each, and conversely, that the fullest development of each is the condition for the full development of all. This core value has huge implications for educational politics and policy, and big implications for curriculum and teaching as well, for what is taught and how.

Democratic teaching is sustained through a culture of respect and mutual recognition that encourages students to develop the capacity to name the world for themselves, to identify the obstacles to their (and other people's) full humanity, and the courage to act upon whatever the known demands. This kind of education is necessarily eye-popping and mind-blowing—always about opening doors and opening minds as students forge their own pathways into a wider, shared world.

But much of what we call schooling is disrespectful of students, parents, and teachers alike—it dishonors their deepest desires and most pressing purposes, it undermines reverence in its basic workings, for example, by rendering these workings opaque through the toxic habit of labeling, sorting, and categorizing on the basis of anemic assumptions and fraudulent science. It blinds us to perspective and process and point-of-view, locks us into well-lit prisons of linear ideas, forecloses or shuts down or walls us off from options and alternatives, and from anything resembling meaningful choice making. Much of schooling enacts a hollowed out ethics and presents an unlovely aesthetic. When schooling is based on

LESSON ONE: REVERENCE

obedience and conformity it reminds us that these qualities and dispositions are the hallmarks of every authoritarian regime throughout history. When schooling suppresses the imagination, banishes the unpopular, squirms in the presence of the unorthodox, and hides the unpleasant, it becomes cowardly, dishonest, and immoral. When schooling segregates and excludes and isolates—whether along racial and ethnic lines or class backgrounds or ability—it fails as the deeply humanizing enterprise it might yet become. We lose, then, our capacity for skepticism, doubt, and imagination. When schooling is simply training, all the ingredients for reverence are quashed and sacrificed.

While many teachers and students long for schooling as something transcendent and powerful, we find ourselves too often locked in institutions that reduce learning to a mindless and irrelevant routine of "drill 'n skill/sit 'n git," and teaching to a kind of glorified clerking, passing along a curriculum of received wisdom and predigested (and mostly false) bits of information. This is unlovely in practice, and it is unworthy of our deepest dreams.

The dominant metaphor in education today posits schools as businesses, teachers as workers, students as products and commodities, and it leads rather simply to thinking that school closings and privatizing the public space are natural events, relentless standardized test-and-punish regimes sensible, zero tolerance a reasonable proxy for justice—this is what the true-believers call "reform."

In this metaphoric strait-jacket, school learning is a lot like boots or hammers. Unlike boots and hammers, the value of which is inherently satisfying and directly understood, the value of school learning is elusive and indirect. Its value, we're assured, has been calculated elsewhere by wise and accomplished people, and these masters know better than anyone what's best for the kids and for the world. "Take this medicine," students are told repeatedly, day after tedious day; "It's good for you." Refuse the bitter pill, and go stand in the corner—where all the other losers are assembled. Schools for obedience and conformity are characterized by passivity and fatalism, insult and injury, and are infused with anti-intellectualism and irrelevance. They turn on the little technologies for control and normalization—the elaborate schemes for managing the mob, the knotted system of rules and discipline, the exhaustive machinery of schedules and clocks, the laborious programs of sorting the crowd into winners and losers through testing and punishing, grading, assessing, and judging, all of it adding up to a familiar darkened cave, an intricately constructed hierarchy—everyone in a designated place and a place for everyone. In the schools as they are, knowing and accepting one's pigeonhole on the towering and barren cliff becomes the only lesson one really needs.

If we hope to foreground reverence in teaching, and contribute to rescuing education from the tangle of its discontents, we must rearticulate and reignite—and try to live out in our daily lives—the proposition that all human beings are of limitless value; and this points inevitably to the understanding that education must be geared toward and powered by the profoundly radical idea mentioned above: the fullest development of all human beings—regardless of race or ethnicity, origin or background, ability or disability—is the necessary condition for the full development of each person, and, conversely, the fullest development of each one is necessary for the full development of all.

This points to the importance of opposing the hidden curriculum of obedience and conformity in favor of foregrounding and teaching initiative, questioning, doubt, skepticism, courage, imagination, invention, and creativity—these are central and not peripheral to an education worthy of free and enlightened human beings. These are qualities we must find ways to model and nourish, encourage and defend in our communities and our classrooms, and they arch toward human rights as a pillar and a standard: "Education shall be directed to the full development of the human personality and to the strengthening of respect for human rights and fundamental freedoms" (Article 26, Universal Declaration of Human Rights).

Reverence in a just and free society encourages everyone to be able to think for themselves and develop minds of their own, to make judgments based on evidence and argument, and to build capacities for imagination and exploration and invention. The most fundamental and essential questions are natural to the young, and like them, these questions are always in-motion, dynamic, and never twice the same: Who in the world am I? How did I get here and where am I going? What in the world are my choices and my chances? What do we know now? What do we have the right to imagine and expect? Who decides? Who's left out? What are the alternatives? What did I learn that the teacher didn't know? Why? What's my story, and how is it like or unlike the stories of others? What is my responsibility to those others? In many ways these kinds of questions are themselves the answers, for they lead us toward a powerful sense that we can and will make a difference. Keeping these questions vital, alive, and fresh is a huge challenge as we search for ways to live within and beyond the contingent and partial answers, as well as the setbacks, discovered and encountered along the way. If we cannot reasonably ask these kinds of questions, and then notice or invent alternatives, we are not free; if we cannot dwell in possibility, we are not fully alive.

Educators who are oriented toward reverence and enlightenment, joy and justice, peace and liberation as living forces and powerful aspirations focus their efforts not on the production of things, but on the production of fully developed human beings who are capable of controlling and transforming their own lives, citizens and residents who can participate actively in public life, people who can open their eyes and awaken themselves and others as they think and act ethically in a complex and ever-changing world. This kind of teaching encourages students to develop initiative and imagination, the capacity to name and constantly interrogate the world, the wisdom to identify the obstacles to their full humanity and to the humanity of others, and the courage to act upon whatever the known demands. Education, then, is transformed from rote learning and endlessly alienating routines into something that is eye-popping and mind-blowing—always opening doors and opening minds as students forge their own pathways into a wider world.

All children need to develop a sense of the unique capacity of human beings to shape and create reality in concert with conscious purposes and plans. This means that our schools—both within and way beyond the existing institutional spaces called "school"—need to be transformed to provide children ongoing opportunities to exercise their resourcefulness, to solve the real problems of their communities, to imagine and invent. Like all human beings, children and young people need to be of use—they cannot productively be treated as "objects" to be taught "subjects." Their cognitive juices will begin to flow if and when their hearts, heads, and hands are engaged in improving their daily lives and their surroundings.

Imagine how much safer and livelier and more peaceful our neighborhoods and communities would become if we reorganized education in a fundamental way—instead of trying to keep children isolated in classrooms, envision engaging them in community-building activities with the same audacity and vision with which the Black Freedom Movement engaged them in desegregation work forty-five years ago: planting community gardens, recycling waste, creating alternative transportation and work sites, naming and protesting injustices around them, organizing neighborhood arts and health festivals, broadcasting a radio show, researching the local waste system, rehabbing houses, painting public murals. By giving children and young people a reason to learn beyond the individualistic goal of getting a job and making more money, by encouraging them to exercise their minds and their hearts and their soul power, we would tap into the deep well of human values that gives life a richer shape and meaning.

Instead of trying to bully young people to remain in classrooms isolated from the community and structured only to prepare them for a distant and quickly disappearing and hostile job market, we might recognize that the reason so many young people drop out from schools is because they are voting with their feet against an educational system that sorts, tracks, tests, and rejects or certifies them like products in a factory. They are crying out for an experience that will value them as human beings.

We ought to be always mindful of the plea in Gwendolyn Brooks's poem "Boy Breaking Glass" (1967a) where she concludes "But I shall create" that is the fundamental and primal cry of the young, and of every human being. A basic challenge to teachers, then, is to stay wide-awake to the world, to the concentric circles of context in which we live and work. Teachers must know and care about some aspect of our shared life—our calling after all is to shepherd and enable the callings of others. Teachers, then, invite students to become somehow more capable, more thoughtful and powerful in their choices, more engaged. More free. More creative. More ethical. More reverent.

Toward the end of Amin Maalouf's dazzling *Samarkand*, a historical novel of the life of Omar Khayam and the journey of the *Rubiayat*, Howard Baskerville, a British school teacher in the city of Tabriz in old Persia at the time of the first democratic revolution, explains an incident in which, stirred by a sense of reverence, Baskerville was observed weeping in the marketplace: "Crying is not a recipe for anything," he begins. "Nor is it a skill. It is simply a naked, naïve and pathetic gesture." But, he goes on, crying is nonetheless important. When the people saw him crying they figured that he "had thrown off the sovereign indifference of a foreigner," and at that moment they could come to Baskerville "to tell me confidentially that crying serves no purpose and that Persia does not need any extra mourners and that the best I could do would be to provide the children of Tabriz with an adequate education." "If they had not seen me crying," Baskerville concludes, "they would never have let me tell the pupils that this Shah was rotten and that the religious chiefs of Tabriz were hardly any better!" (1998, 230).

The great Persian poet Rumi writes: "Why should I seek? I am the same as He. His essence speaks through me. I have been looking for myself!" Teaching occurs in context, and pedagogy and technique are not the wellsprings of moral choice. Teaching becomes reverence when it is guided by an unshakable commitment to working with human beings to reach the full measure of their humanity, and a willingness to reach toward a future fit for all, a world we can only imagine. The fundamental message of the teacher is this: You can change your life! A necessary corollary: You must change the world!

Education is in part a matter of opening the creative vent, the inventive and the productive option, so that alternatives can be seen and chosen, so that the destructive can be challenged and even closed. This leads us to the precincts of the arts in their many incarnations.

High School Haiku[1]
school—
take out the "sh"
and it's cool

Gwendolyn Brooks asked in her poem "The Chicago Picasso" (1967b), written in response to the installation of a sculpture by Picasso in that city, "Does man love art?" Her answer: "Man visits art but squirms. Art hurts. Art urges voyages." Art, which often begins in pain and horror, and when it is good art, ends in the imaginable, embraces the entire territory of possibility. Art stands next to the world as such, the given or the received world, waving a colorful flag gesturing toward a world that should be, or a world that could be but is not yet. So if we believe that the world is perfect and in need of no improvement, or that the world is none of our business, or that we are at the end of history and that this is as good as it gets and that no repair is possible, then we must banish the arts, cuff and gag the artists—remember, they urge voyages. If, on the other hand, we feel a responsibility to engage and participate, then the arts are our strongest ally.

Perhaps that's what Ferlinghetti was thinking when he published a slim volume with the provocative title *Poetry as Insurgent Art*, or what Picasso had in mind when he said, "Art is not chaste. Those ill-prepared should be allowed no contact with art. Art is dangerous. If it is chaste it is not art." Add to that Einstein's famous observation that "Imagination is more important than knowledge. For knowledge is limited to all we now know and understand, while imagination embraces the entire world, and all there ever will be to know and understand." Everyone is on the move and on the make, propulsive, dynamic, unsettled, and alive.

Gwendolyn Brooks was a public intellectual and a well-known, fully engaged resident of Chicago's storied South Side, and she was a teacher, as well, with a huge following of both students and admirers. Her notable and most widely anthologized poem is, "The Pool Players Seven at the Golden Shovel" or more commonly, "We Real Cool." Haki Madhubuti, Gwendolyn Brooks' publisher as well as her artistic son, claims that art is a "prodigious and primary energy source," and then turns to the connection of art to education: "Children's active participation...is what makes them whole, significantly human, secure in their own skin" (2002, 129). His poem then becomes a chant, each line ending with the words "with art" or "through art" (129–130). Every teacher or student, parent or community member can play along and add on: magnify your children's mind with art, jumpstart their questions... keep their young minds running, jumping, and excited... Keep them off drugs, respecting themselves and others, away from war... with art! Reverence and teaching, liberation and freedom, enlightenment and morality call us again and again to the arts.

Note

1. The following section has been adapted from my blog entry entitled "High School Haiku," published June 26, 2010: http://billayers.wordpress.com/2010/06/26/high-school-haiku/

References

Brooks G. 1967a. "Boy Breaking Glass." http://www.poetryfoundation.org/poem/172094.

———. 1967b. "Two Dedications—The Chicago Picasso and The Wall." http://faculty.chemeketa.edu/jrupert3/eng255/Resources/gwenpoem.htm.

Cofer, J. O. 1995. *Reaching for the Mainland and Selected New Poems.* Tempe, AZ: Bilingual Press.

Maalouf, A. 1998. *Samarkand.* Translated by Russell Harris. New York: Interlink Books.

Madhubuti, H. R. 2002. "Art: Nurturing Exceptional Children." In *Tough Notes: A Healing Call for Creating Exceptional Black Men,* 127–131. Chicago: Third World Press.

Rumi. http://www.numii.net/word_press/gurus/rumi.

Universal Declaration of Human Rights. http://www.un.org/en/documents/udhr/index.shtml#a26.

9

Quotidian Sublimity

Megan J. Laverty

> Awe...is the beginning of metaphysics.
>
> —*Charles Simic (1990, 88)*

A person could be forgiven for linking reverence to religion and organized worship. It is widely believed that as a capacity for awe and wonder, reverence should be inspired by that which is beyond human comprehension and control. This power is traditionally conceived as a divine and essentially mysterious being or God. In other words, reverence implies the existence of something in light of which humans come to understand themselves as flawed, limited, or "fallen." Such an understanding dissuades individuals from behaving like gods and inspires them to treat others as God's creatures; it diminishes the ego and promotes compassionate, respectful regard for others. Reverent humans "know their place" in a world divinely ordained, ultimately transcendent, and essentially mysterious.

The idea that reverence entails a belief in the existence of whatever inspires our experience of it makes perfect sense, but it can leave us feeling unable to account for much of life. It may make us want to return to the consideration of plain and simple truths.[1] I attempt such a return by reflecting on two truths. First, that essential mysteriousness is commonplace. While much of our experience is conventional, some of it is not. We brood on past experiences; we struggle to convey what we feel and speak about pain only with great difficulty; we marvel at our lovers, friends, and family. Second, reverence is more like a quality of ordinary consciousness. We are at our most reverent when absorbed in disciplined concentration. When we attend to something intently—whether caring for a new baby, mastering a musical technique, or preparing a meal—we bring reality into focus as our entire being is focused by that reality.

Like Paul Woodruff (2001), I view reverence as a morally significant attitude that is not necessarily related to religion. Whereas Woodruff draws on ancient Greek and Chinese texts, I turn toward Immanuel Kant and Iris Murdoch's arguments for a transcendent, essentially mysterious and necessarily real alternative to God. Kant calls this alternative Reason and Murdoch calls it the Good. We discover this reality through awe or *Achtung* in Kant's terms. Kant and Murdoch identify this experience as the sublime. It is when an individual encounters a limit to human consciousness *as* he or she intuits a transcendent, nonrepresentable reality. It is as if the individual is able to reach out and touch reality at the very moment that his or her consciousness fails to comprehend reality. Kant locates the sublime in the contemplation of nature, whereas Murdoch locates it in the experience of reading great literature. In both cases the sublime elevates the soul and saves us from despair by arousing a moral interest.

Kant introduces an idea of the sublime that Murdoch develops. Kant associates the sublime with an intuition of Reason. Having already established that Reason is humanity's noumenal reality—it is that supersensible faculty that confers upon us free moral agency as our true destiny—Kant argues that it is *only* by witnessing the relative greatness of nature's size and strength that individuals are given necessary experiential proof of humanity's absolute greatness. Although we may not be able to comprehend nature's size or resist its force, we can conceive of such moral ideas as "infinity" and "eternity." Reason is humanity's true measure and uniquely inspires *Achtung*. The sublime energizes individuals to pursue their supersensible destiny by acting solely from duty.

Murdoch associates the sublime with the intuition of a particular. Particulars provide random experiential proof that something rather than nothing exists. Sometimes, particulars inexplicably pierce consciousness, as in the case of an individual transfixed by "a hovering kestrel."[2] At other times, particulars are "the result" of disciplined and loving attention directed toward an individual reality, as in the case of learning a new language.[3] These instances demonstrate that reverence can be commanded in the form of "those little efforts of imagination which have such cumulative results" (Murdoch 1970, 43). In either case, the sublime inspires awe as well as gratitude and fidelity: we want to focus on what is not ourselves, become more attuned to a separately existing reality and to allow it condition understanding.

Murdoch's idea of the sublime is important within the context of education as I shall demonstrate in this chapter. We all recognize schooling as an experience that is far from being exalted. Students spend most of their time confined within uninspiring buildings, routinely moving between classrooms, completing worksheets, and performing tests. Schooling can, and should be, improved. It would be regrettable, however, if participation in the organized social life of schools prevented students from apprehending the mystery of existence. Educators should strive to develop ways to heighten students' experience. Such imperatives provide the deepest motives and aims of education.

This chapter is divided into three parts. In the first part, I discuss the South Korean film *Poetry* (2010). The film explores the unfathomable beauty of ordinary existence and the moral imperative for us to find ways to appreciate it. In the second part, I explain Kant and Murdoch on the sublime, elaborating how Murdoch improves upon Kant's original idea. In the third part, I conclude by introducing two pedagogical practices: writing and conversation. The pedagogies themselves are not new but consideration of them within the cultivation of reverence and moral judgment is.

The Question of Reverence Explored through *Poetry*

Woodruff claims that reverence has been forgotten but he could just as likely be mistaken about this. A person might argue that reverence has rightly been discarded as an antiquated and superfluous virtue. After all, there seems to be little that is beyond human comprehension and control. Contemporary scientific discoveries and technological advances make the idea of reverence increasingly unintelligible and obscure. Furthermore, reverence seems contrary to our democratic, egalitarian spirit. Respect, a healthy and nonpathological regard for others as equals, seems a more appropriate virtue for living in a democracy. A case needs to be made for contemporary viability of reverence and I interpret the film, *Poetry*, as doing just that.

The film's central character, Mija Yang (Jeong-hie Yun), is a sixty-six-year-old grandmother diagnosed with Alzheimer's disease. She lives on government welfare that she supplements by working as a part-time maid. Mija cares for her grandson, Wook Jong (Lee David), whose divorced mother lives in Busan. Early on, Mija registers for a one-month poetry course at the local community center. She is to write one poem to be submitted at the end of the course. The instructor tells the students that in order to write poetry they must really see well. They must seek true beauty everywhere and this is not just what appears beautiful. He assures them that poetic inspiration can be found in the most menial activities and surroundings, including even a dishwashing basin. Mija struggles valiantly for poetic inspiration and decides to attend the local poetry reading evenings to learn more.

The story of Mija's fourteen-year-old grandson, Wook, is told alongside that of her creative writing pursuits. The camera does not "follow" Wook. Rather this fairly typical, if unlikable, teenager is observed only in his interactions with Mija. He is technologically literate, and morally illiterate. Slovenly, ill-mannered, unceremonious, and insistent upon his own material needs, he eats in front of the television, entertains his friends in his bedroom, and begrudges time spent with his grandmother. Mija tolerates her grandson's behavior until she discovers that he has, along with five male friends, been repeatedly raping a female student, Agnes Park Heejin. It had gone on for six months until the girl's suicide. The film opens with an extended and silent shot of the girl's body slowly floating down the river. The grandmother dutifully conspires with the fathers of the other young men to pay off the girl's mother 30 million Won to keep her quiet. She has to blackmail her elderly employer for her share.

Mija is pained by what her grandson has done and by his lack of remorse. She confronts Wook repeatedly, and in different emotional registers, but he remains unmoved. Mija undertakes a pilgrimage to discover the spirit of the dead girl. She visits the science laboratory where the rape took place; attends a Requiem Mass; brings home a photograph of Agnes to display on the kitchen table; travels to the bridge from which Agnes jumped; and visits Agnes' grieving mother without disclosing her identity. Never having met Agnes, Mija is trying to piece together a portrait of the deceased girl from her lasting traces in photographs, spaces she once inhabited, and the life of her mother. Mija is striving to make sense of a situation that threatens her very power of comprehension. In order to understand the situation Mija must revise what she considered to be the fabric of her world; she must come to see a different world.

After paying off the mother, Mija decides to report her grandson's crime to the local chief of police. Without telling Wook of her decision, Mija calls his mother asking her to come the next day. She takes Wook out to dinner, insisting that he bath and dress decently. She challenges him to a game of evening badminton so that she will be with him when the police officers arrive. The next day, Mija leaves her poem and a bouquet of flowers for the poetry instructor. Mija's poem, "Agnes' Song," does not clearly identify the speaking voice. It could be Agnes addressing her deceased father before her suicide or, it could be Mija addressing Agnes as she contemplates her own suicide.[4] This question is left unresolved. In the very last shot of the film, however, Agnes gazes directly into the camera as though to affirm her overwhelming presence.

The film asks us to consider whether Mija would have come to her decision had she not been in the poetry course. Mija's movement between participating in the poetry course and attending to her grandson's affairs provides the dialectic of the film. Mija struggles to lucidly reconcile her abiding love for her grandson with the enormity of his unspeakable crime. She struggles to preserve a sense of her life as meaningful but her memory is becoming compromised by Alzheimer's. She can no longer remember the names of simple things. She begins to doubt her role as principal care giver, first to her daughter and then to her grandson. As the meaningfulness of Mija's life is called into question, she is awakened to the preciousness of existence. The students in the poetry course take turns to speak about "The Most Beautiful Moment of my Life." One woman speaks about teaching her grandmother to sing; a man speaks about moving to an apartment having lived in a basement for twenty years; another woman speaks about falling in love with a married man; another speaks about giving birth at forty; and Mija recalls her first memory and the sensation of knowing that she was truly loved. The overall impression is one of rich diversity and historical contingency.

These stories punctuate the film providing points of contrast to Wook's life. As far as it is possible to judge, Wook lives life like an arcade game, ruthlessly strategizing about opportunities and obstacles. Powerlessness is a constant source of frustration for him. Neglected by his mother, Wook lives in a small apartment with his poor and uneducated grandmother, dividing his time between home, school, and the video arcade. The point is that Mija's life is no different. She divides her time between the apartment, community center, and place of employment. Her life is nearly over and she had none of the opportunities and advantages open to Wook. The difference is that while always civil and ceremonious, Mija attends to the real beauty of the objects and people surrounding her. She seeks to be drawn into responsive communication with whatever is present. Mija assumes greater responsibility for her consciousness, no longer allowing it to proceed in a blandly conformist manner. It gradually dawns on Mija that she does not have to follow the conventional thinking regarding her grandson either. She begins to look for a response that is necessitated by the situation. In the end she feels compelled to report her grandson's crime and possibly—it remains unclear from the film—commit suicide.

Mija decides upon an unprecedented course of action: she subjugates her concern for her grandson and resists the desire to shield him from harm. Mija suspects that her concern is "*faulty*" (Diamond 1991, 316). She doubts that concern for grandson's welfare has allowed her to truly see, and think about, *him*. It dawns on Mija that Wook has a life that *only he* can live and that he must begin to take responsibility for its imaginative and real possibilities. Mija hopes that Wook will come to convert elements of his own circumstances into "the stuff of adventure" as she has learned (ibid., 314). "Adventure" is a word that Cora Diamond uses to describe the moral life, specifically to convey a "sense of life lived in a world of wonderful possibilities, but possibilities to be found only by creative response" (ibid., 313). Mija is morally creative in the sense that she improvises a course of action that is both unforeseen *and* necessary. Indeed, watching the coordination of Wook's arrest, his mother's arrival, and Mija's departure gives the viewer the impression of being inside a living poem.

The film suggests that Mija learns from writing poetry that situations, things, and individuals are always greater than what we can ever know of them; they contain unfathomable depths, essential mysteries and unbidden surprises. The mysteriousness of situations, things, and individuals is disclosed only under a certain imaginative pressure. The film works to establish "a kind of transforming perception" connected to moral creativity and seeing unprecedented possibilities (ibid., 313). Mija applies imaginative pressure to her situation—as well as to her surroundings—to discover a moral possibility that, while responding to the present also integrates her past. Philosophical treatments of the sublime provide some explanation for this link between a transforming perception and conceiving moral possibility, as the following section will demonstrate.

The Sublime Revisited: Kant and Murdoch

Kant and Murdoch assert that reality exists but it cannot be known; reality is intuited or discerned. "Noumenal" and "supersensible" are terms Kant uses to describe reality and "formless" is Murdoch's. Although essentially mysterious, reality surrenders its "truths" on certain occasions. Kant is more prescriptive about these occasions than Murdoch.[5] In the *Critique of Judgment* he differentiates between ordinary (determinant and interested) and aesthetic (reflective disinterested) experience. He further divides aesthetic experience into the beautiful (free and dependent) and the sublime (mathematical and dynamical). In ordinary experience, individuals subsume particulars under preexisting concepts, projects, and desires. In aesthetic experience, the particular is simply given: it inspires the individual to seek a concept that best captures how he or she feels. The feeling must be spontaneous and unmediated; and yet, the judgment distinguishes itself from mere preference by claiming subjective universality.

Feelings distinguish the beautiful from the sublime. If the experience of an object inspires delight or pleasure, apart from any involvement of a concept or interest, then it is judged beautiful. Pleasure results from the harmonizing free play of understanding and imagination. Objects capable of producing the harmonizing free play of faculties include: a bird's song, plain music (without words), trees, flowers, flower beds, gardens, wallpaper patterns, and decorative drawing. In an experience of the sublime, an individual will oscillate between feelings of extreme displeasure and pleasure. Displeasure occurs because understanding and imagination fail. An individual either fails to comprehend the sheer size of the natural universe (the mathematical sublime); or, the individual fails to imagine how to resist the powerful force of nature (dynamical sublime).

The failure of understanding and imagination throws into relief Reason, the third and only remaining faculty. With consciousness momentarily disarmed, the individual intuits the absolute superiority of the good or free will. While consciousness may fail to comprehend and control noumenal reality, noumenal reality reasserts itself in the unqualified freedom of human agency or Reason. Reason is supersensible and thus it inspires *Achtung*, translated as reverence, awe, or respect. Reverence *is* being awakened to the presence of Reason; it is the discovery of the necessity and unrealizability of humanity's moral destiny. Reason is the source of moral ideas, such as "infinity," "eternity," and "justice." Without these ideas the sublime would merely strike the individual "as terrifying" (Kant 1991, 115). Although humans are relatively small and weak compared to nature, our absolute greatness resides in our Reason, our ability to conceive of justice and act accordingly. No object can be sublime; it is only certain aspects of our nature (Reason) that occasion feelings of sublimity in us. Kant writes that "[w]hen we are confronted with the overwhelmingly powerful, the weakness of our empirical selves makes us aware of our worth as moral beings" (ibid., 131).

Kant's thinking on the sublime finds its fullest expression in the paintings of Caspar David Friedrich, particularly *Wanderer Above the Sea of Fog* (1818) and *Monk by the Sea* (1809). Both present a solitary man against a vast and impressive landscape. In *Monk by the Sea*, a small figure surveys the broad expanse of sea and sky. In *Wanderer Above the Sea of Fog*, a man is poised on an Alpine precipice, looking out into the distance over clouds and rugged mountains. Both paintings capture the hero's physical insignificance, his intense solitude and profound vulnerability. They create an impression of contemplative dignity that rescues the hero from abject humiliation. The greater the violence and solitude, the more striking the hero's preeminence. The towering mountains, vast skies, and endless seas are symbolically transfigured as natural greatness comes to imagine true greatness. Our feeling of awe is redirected from the majestic sweep of the landscape to the seemingly insignificant, solitary hero.

The sublime sets a clear standard for what humans need to do if they are to realize their greatness. Individuals must eschew baseness (empirical motives) in the interests of purity (acting from duty). To act from duty is to respect the moral law and to respect the moral law is to accept its unconditional worth. The unconditional worth of the moral law thwarts any self-related interests, desires, and aspirations, making it exceedingly difficult to establish good will. Kant acknowledges that it may be impossible for any individual to act from pure duty. The unrealizability of the moral law, however, does not diminish its authority. As a regulative ideal, the moral law illuminates our ascetical path; we are as less than perfect.

Murdoch admires Kant's idea of the sublime, as "one of the most beautiful and exciting things in the whole of philosophy" (1997, 212). She "cannot help brooding upon the relation of sublimity to *Achtung* and feeling that it must be pregnant with something marvelous" (ibid., 213). She complains, however, that "Kant's man stands alone confronting the mountains or the sea and feels defiant pride in the free power of his reason" (ibid., 283). Here Murdoch criticizes Kant for attaching the sublime to what she considers to be a relatively "trivial occasion": regarding the phenomena of the natural world from atop the European Alps (ibid., 264). She holds that such a restriction of the sublime forces that self-directed enjoyment of nature exhibited by Romantic poets and painters. Murdoch's second criticism is leveled at Kant's claim that reverence cannot be commanded and that it is uniquely inspired by Reason. In the case of the sublime, the individual's admiration for the relative greatness of nature is transformed into reverence for the absolute greatness of humanity. Reason assures us of our moral destiny and affirms our exalted self-importance.

Murdoch doubts the truth of Kant's version of the sublime because it appeals to the ego's fantasy mechanism. Kant's sublime is dangerously intoxicating and elitist. In Plato's terms, Kant is looking at the fire and not the sun. The individual is turned inward rather than outward. Murdoch's concern is that the "self is such a dazzling object that if one looks *there* one may see nothing else" (1970, 30). Murdoch accuses Kant of replacing death with suffering. According to Murdoch, humans find it extremely difficult to contemplate death. Death is inscribed in all aspects of life and can occur at any moment of our existence. It makes helpless, transient creatures of us all. Few individuals can bear the magnitude of such an inescapable fact. Death is a void. Suffering, on the contrary, is intense, exhilarating, complex, and "far too interesting" (ibid., 68). It appeals to our sadomasochistic tendencies. Death equalizes whereas suffering instills hierarchy. Suffering admits of degrees and only a brave or enlightened few can fully subject themselves to its imposing demands (Murdoch 1992).

Murdoch offers a corrective vision of the sublime. She cautions against giving any organized sense of reality. She agrees with Kant that humans make sense of their experience by falsifying whatever they disclose. She also agrees that they intuit reality in the form of the sublime. Her characterization of the sublime, however, depicts it as not all that enthralling or dramatic; and the reality we intuit is not designated by a special faculty that secures human ascendancy. According to Murdoch, the sublime is "the apprehension of something else, something particular, as existing outside us" (1997, 216). To apprehend a particular is to see what makes the thing itself. The individual discovers that there is something instead of nothing. We can experience existence while reading a novel, watching a kestrel, weeding the garden, or sweeping the floor. Reverence comes from or rather *is* the perception of existence. Recalling a phrase from Wittgenstein, Murdoch writes: "It is not 'how' things are in the world that is mystical, but that it exists" (1970, 85).

Murdoch criticizes Kant for his fear of particulars: their messiness, incompleteness, arbitrariness, and historicity. She claims that anything can be a particular: "the resistant otherness of other persons, other things, history, the natural world, [and] the cosmos" (1992, 268). The shining particularity of *this* table or *this* tree pierces an individual's consciousness, striking into him or her like a beam of light. The individual is awakened to a reality that exceeds human comprehension and control. An absolute limit to human consciousness is discovered, but the individual does not set out on the path of becoming truly human. The origin of the limit is more modest and, at the same time, great. Existence necessitates that we simply let other things be, in their rich diversity and specificity. The perception of existence against a background of nothingness—death and chance—stimulates us to consider what is not ourselves in a spirit of humble gratitude.

Murdoch thinks that of all the particulars, people are the most resistant. She writes: "Other people are, after all, the most interesting features of our world and in some way the most poignantly and mysteriously alien" (Murdoch 1997, 257). She concludes, contra Kant, that individuals should look "not at the Alps, but at the spectacle of human life" (ibid., 282). Her belief is that the spectacle of human life "brings the exhilaration and the power and reminds us, to use Kant's words, of our supersensible destiny" (ibid.). Reading great literature reminds us of our supersensible destiny because novelists "*reveal* an aspect of the world which no other art can," namely "that other people exist." They reorient us toward the reality of other people by illuminating that understanding them "does not come to an end." Novels promote agnostic tolerance toward other individuals as separate centers of meaning and encourage us to be more respectful and compassionate toward them.

Murdoch's vision of the sublime has important implications for education. She holds that individuals need not go beyond what they ordinarily do to "touch" reality. Individuals are more inclined to encounter the limit of consciousness and glimpse reality while reading a letter, viewing a painting, or sitting in a garden, since these experiences can act as conduits of the sublime. A significant feature of these experiences is that they are made possible by the creative acts of ordinary individuals, not all that dissimilar from us: strangers, neighbors, amateurs, gardeners, writers, and artists. Thus, these experiences can serve to instruct us in how to exercise our own partial freedom by disciplining consciousness. In Murdoch's terms, these experiences teach "how real things can be looked at and loved without being seized and used" (1970, 65).

Amateurs, gardeners, letter-writers, artists, and the like do not disavow consciousness; instead, they seek to make it more obedient. They seek to know things through how those things claim us. They aspire to "a refined and honest perception of what is really the case, a patient and just discernment and exploration of what confronts one" (ibid., 39). Murdoch uses the word "attention" to describe it. She takes the word from Simone Weil and uses it to express "the idea of a just and loving gaze directed upon an individual reality" (ibid., 34). It is to the teaching of attention that I turn to in the next part.

Contemplation and Conversation

Weil argues that teaching should aim to simply train attention. While Weil defends the value of disciplined study in this regard, I want to focus on some extracurricular activities. Such a focus is an advantage in the current educational climate with its emphasis on standardized testing. The activities that I have in mind involve words or, more specifically, using words in a living engagement with our surroundings and one another. It may seem odd to propose that we teach attention by examining words. Language, however, is the "stuff" of consciousness and as the "stuff" of consciousness words are all that we have to "express ourselves into existence" (Murdoch 1997, 241). We should not be overly impressed by words, but they are nonetheless significant. I agree with Weil: "Intelligence can never penetrate the mystery, but it, and it alone, can judge of the suitability of the words which express it. For this task it needs to be keener, more discerning, more precise, more exact and more exacting than for any other" (Weil 1987, 118). Although language and thought are not completely coextensive, to *see* the world differently is to describe it differently and vice versa. Sometimes our words remain unaltered as our concepts deepen to illuminate a reality previously not apprehended.

For these reasons it is important to allow students to write and talk about the world *as they see it*. Unfortunately, students often learn writing as an abstract and discrete subject. They learn a range of writing conventions that they practice across different assignments, confident that they are developing an invaluable academic and professional skill. Such an approach to writing obscures its roots in human association and interaction. The value of having students write and talk about the world, as they see it, is that it returns writing to its origins in personal experience, reflection, and communication.

Along these lines, we might ask students to consciously collect and write down their memorable images. It would not be very different from the poetry instructor asking his students to recall and describe the most beautiful moment they have experienced. The value of images is they are intimate vehicles of transcendence: like a favorite painting, an empty classroom, the view from one's backdoor, or a dog who waits patiently on the windowsill. Sometimes, our images fade, become transformed or, transform their meaning only many years later. It is important for students to describe their images in words: in prose, poetry, or aphorisms. Such exercises encourage them to express, with the greatest honesty and precision, how things are. How things are incorporates the significance the student sees them as having that, in turn, incorporates how the student experiences them. Students need to be made aware that no word will be completely adequate to the task and, therefore, they are not failing where others have succeeded. Nonetheless they will learn quickly that not every word is as good as another.

In this writing exercise students should be discouraged from narration and interpretation. The aim is to sustain being present in the process of writing about presence. It is to bring reality to bear upon the very capacity that prevents us from joining it, finding ways to say with language what cannot be put into words. It is, in Heidegger's terms, thinking as thanking (Heidegger 1968). To describe what we find within the context of how it strikes us. In the film, *Poetry*, Mija initially despairs of finding words to capture her experiences. She doubts that she even has experiences. As she begins to find the words for her experiences—sometimes as simple as "flowers and blood"—she also becomes more aware of, and available to, experience. She lifts her face to the sun; she leans her body back to enjoy the warm breeze; and she lingers by the river allowing the water pass through her fingers. The challenge of describing these experiences awakens Mija to her own individuality. It slowly dawns on her that she does not have to follow the conventional thinking regarding her grandson. She realizes that she must find a response that is necessary *for her*.

These writing assignments need not be assessed, but they could be shared in conversation. There is such tremendous variety where conversation is concerned: some conversations are thoughtful and others thoughtless; no two conversations are alike; we can converse with just about anyone about anything. Conversations remind us of the living nature of language, allowing for the improvisation of grammatical authority as meanings are sought, offered, tested, and revised. Put differently, conversations create commonality. They alleviate isolation, but not in a purely psychological sense. Conversations bring individuals into a world of shared significance and, therefore, experience. In the film *Poetry*, Mija's isolation is accentuated by her conspicuous silence. She has conversations, but they are only in passing and do not draw her out. The poetry evenings involve her in a community of individuals who share a love of poetry. It is through and listening to one another's poems that these individuals come to appreciate and share significance. It is not surprising that Mija should lose her dignified composure on one such evening. She withdraws to an outdoor area just behind the restaurant and to give herself over to quiet weeping. She is discovered by the local chief of police who is enjoying a cigarette. Earlier in the evening, Mija had expressed distaste for his poetry, characterizing it as ugly and crude. We do not witness their conversation and are left wondering about what might have transpired between these two very different personalities.

Conversations teach that meanings are not predetermined givens transmitted from person to person. They are created, pluralized, and made common through a process of constant interaction and revision. We are inclined to take our concepts for granted but we discover quickly that others conceive and use words differently from us. Conversations inspire as much uncertainty as they do connection. Conversational partners doubt they have mutually understood one another. One hears such comments as "I have never experienced grief, what is it like?" or "I wouldn't call *that* friendship!" or "I am puzzled you should see it that way." In these examples the calls for meaning divert the conversation from proceeding superficially. Words and concepts cannot be taken as wholly and satisfactorily "given." We have to begin to think about the other person's perspective. In John Dewey's terms, conversational partners must strive "to assimilate, imaginatively, something of another's experience" in order to articulate a thought (1944, 6). Conversations make it impossible for one individual to insist on his or her own thinking and talking as the only way. Individuals must respect one another's equal claim to linguistic authority. It is through the improvisatory and shared process of conversation that meanings are enhanced and deepened. Thus Dewey asserts that "man is lifted from his immediate isolation and shares in a communion of meanings" (1929, 205).

Language is not the only means by which meaning is conveyed in conversation. Facial expressions and gestures play important roles. Gesture is a human response to the presence of another individual. As people, we address, and are addressed by, one another all the time. The significance of such an interaction is that it draws the addresser and the addressee into a responsive communication before they even know what their communication is to be about. It is the moment of being present to one another before the insertion of respective personalities, projects, and history. It demarcates a larger, living context for their conversation.

I am suggesting, in the tradition of Dewey and others, that students be given the opportunity to engage in conversations. These conversations need not occur in the classroom or among students of the same year level; instead, they should be between individuals from across the school community. These conversations will be replete with false-starts, awkward interchanges, subtle and not so subtle conflicts, and mild confusion. I would rather this than the construal of them as educationally purposeful. While these conversations most likely contribute to the education of citizenship or character, this is not their principal office. First and foremost, these conversations are an occasion of presence; individuals address, and are addressed by, one another. Furthermore, they provide an occasion for individuals to share and interrogate what they see. "See" here refers to a reality understood "in relation to the progressing life of the person" (Murdoch 1970, 26). It is a reality imbued with significance that calls out for our different possibilities. Murdoch cautions that this reality should, "given the variety of human personality and situation only be thought of as 'one,' as a single object for all men, in some very remote and ideal sense" (ibid., 38).

Conclusion

I have focused here on how words are used within particular acts of attention and conversation. It is noteworthy, however, that there are other ways to command reverence. Silently working with one's hands is one such way. For educators, this happens when we fulfill routine "household" tasks: organizing the room at the start and close of each school day; creating points of interest in the classroom, taking down old displays and putting up new ones; rearranging the desks, cubbies, and the supplies. Woodruff would describe these as "countless small acts of ceremony" (2001, 205). I agree with Woodruff that reverence is "often expressed in, and reinforced by, ceremony" that requires our participation in a shared culture (ibid., 63). Woodruff does not view reverence as having the power to disclose reality, other than to remind us of our "human limitations" (ibid., 54). Thus, reverence promotes the respectful treatment for others in recognition of our shared humanity. Here I am inclined to disagree.

Small, seemingly insignificant acts of attention, conversation, and ceremony can provide glimpses of a transcendent, essentially mysterious, and necessary reality. These "very tiny spark[s] of insight" make it possible for us to take imaginative responsibility for consciousness and transform perception (Murdoch 1970, 73). They invite recognition that others are also morally underway. Each individual must discover what is morally necessary for her or him to think and do. This occurs only against a background of moral possibilities that arise out of how the individual experiences the significance of the world.

Individuals are more inclined to experience the significance of the world when they exercise attention. There should be plenty of opportunities throughout the school day for students to exercise and cultivate attention. They can do this in the context of collecting and recording memorable images, engaging their peers in conversation about what they find meaningful, or participating in the small acts of ceremony that contribute to the upkeep of the classroom and school. If we school our students in the sublime, then they may discover the moral possibilities of which we have only dreamed.

Notes

I want to thank Kazuaki Yoda for renewing my interest in Simone Weil and Kyung Hwa Jung for recommending the film *Poetry*. This chapter grew out of my response to Christopher Cordner's review of my book *Iris Murdoch's Ethics: A Consideration of her Romantic Vision* (New York and London: Continuum, 2007). His review is in the *Notre Dame Review of Books*, 2008.06.40: http://ndpr.nd.edu/review.cfm?id=13428. Accessed June 17, 2011.

1. See Murdoch 1970, 1; Murdoch 1997, 242. Also, Zwicky 1992, L41: "The wish to become clear about things outside the domain of science is of course common. The idea that we might use non-systematic means to become clear is less common."
2. "I am looking out of my window in an anxious and resentful state of mind, oblivious of my surroundings, brooding perhaps on some damage done to my prestige. Then suddenly I observe a hovering kestrel. In a moment everything is altered. The brooding self with its hurt vanity has disappeared. There is nothing now but kestrel. And when I return to thinking of the other matter it seems less important." Murdoch 1970, 84.
3. "If I am learning, for instance, Russian, I am confronted by an authoritative structure which commands my respect. The task is difficult and the goal is

distant and perhaps never entirely attainable. My work is a progressive revelation of something which exists independently of me. Attention is rewarded by a knowledge of reality. Love of Russian leads me away from myself towards something alien to me, something which my consciousness cannot take over, swallow up, deny or make unreal." Murdoch 1970, 89.
4. The poem contains questions about the afterlife ("How is over there? Are the birds still singing on the way to forest?"), a confession of profound love and a prayer to meet in the afterlife.
5. Kant wrote two works on aesthetics: *Observations on the Feeling of the Beautiful and the Sublime*, originally published in 1764, and *Critique of Judgment*, published in 1790. My comments draw from the latter.

References

Diamond, C. 1991. "Missing the Adventure: Reply to Martha Nussbaum." In *The Realistic Spirit: Wittgenstein, Philosophy, and the Mind*. Cambridge, MA: MIT Press.
Dewey, J. 1944. *Democracy and Education: An Introduction to the Philosophy of Education*. New York: Free Press.
———. 1929. *Experience and Nature*. London: Allen & Unwin.
Heidegger, M. 1968. *What Is Called Thinking?*, Translated by J. G. Gray. New York: Harper and Row.
Kant, I. 1991. *The Critique of Judgment*. Translated by J. C. Meredith. Oxford: Oxford University Press.
———. 1997. *The Foundations of the Metaphysics of Morals*. Translated by L. W. Beck. Second Edition. Upper Saddle River, NJ: Prentice-Hall.
———. 1981. *Observations on the Feeling of the Beautiful and Sublime*. Edited by J. T. Goldthwait. Berkeley: University of California Press.
Murdoch, I. 1992. *Metaphysics as a Guide to Morals*. London: Chatto & Windus.
———. 1997. *Existentialists and Mystics: Writings on Philosophy and Literature*. Edited by Peter Conradi, 261–286. London: Penguin.
———. 1970. *The Sovereignty of Good*. New York and London: Routledge.
Simic, C. 1990. "Wonderful Words, Silent Truth." In *Wonderful Words, Silent Truth: Essays on Poetry and a Memoir*, 85–95. Ann Arbor: University of Michigan Press.
Weil, Simone. 1987. *Gravity and Grace*. Translated by E. Craufurd. London and New York: Routledge.
Woodruff, P. 2001. *Reverence: Renewing a Forgotten Virtue*. New York: Oxford University Press.
Zwicky, J. 1992. *Lyric Philosophy*. Toronto: University of Toronto Press.

10

Reverence for Things Not Seen: Implied Creators in Works of Art, Implied Teachers in Creative Pedagogy

Bruce Novak

I came to teaching relatively late in life. And in the beginning I was in no way a "natural" teacher. Like many who start in the profession, I was unsure of myself, unsure of my commitment to teaching, unsure I would ever "make it." I had one experience, though, that solidified my relationship with the profession, that showed me that teaching was not just a career I had chosen, but a destiny—a calling that had chosen me and to which I had become inalienably committed.

Toward the end of my student teaching, I designed an activity—the details don't matter here, and I remember barely anything about them anyway—that enabled me simply to sit back and enjoy my students' enjoying of it. A word or two here or there was all I needed to say—the thing I'd made did all the rest. It brought the students alive and brought the material alive for them. I'd created a little world that these people could come to play together in, that also brought a meaningful part of the larger world outside it into imaginative play. And it was *good*. *Very* good. Good enough to stake a life on.

Twenty years down the road now, I've developed a theory to account for the meaning of this experience that I'd like to share with you here. It's a theory, first, of how a certain kind of *mediated* reverence is key both to art and to teaching. Second, it is a theory of how understanding the psychological processes through which this reverence is evoked can help us comprehend both how art teaches and how a certain kind of artistry lies at the heart of teaching. Most importantly, though, and most pertinent to what I see as the ultimate and most important concerns of this book, it is also a theory of how a fuller educative cultivation of this mediated form of reverence can help us find a new reverential religious grounding for democratic life—or, rather, uncover a grounding that has been there all along, and just needs to be broadly acknowledged and deliberately cultivated to be made solid in reality.

As we learn to revere the gifts of the past, not blindly and for their own sake but precisely through perceiving and revering the life *we* are able to *co*create through these gifts, which then keep giving through us, we develop a religious reverence for the mutual self-government that occurs through the bestowal, reception, and perpetuation across time of such personal gifts. Mutual respect for natural rights, which presents a deep challenge to the human soul, is transmuted into mutual reverence for these personal gifts, which is deeply fulfilling to it.

It's not that the phenomena of responsive reciprocation to the personal gifts of teaching and art are not already broadly recognized. A good many of us—mostly teachers and artists of various stripes—already see them, know how to carefully evoke them, and to evoke reverence for their personal and interpersonal importance. But few presently are able to see that the fulfillment offered by this reverence is not necessarily limited to the personal domain. It also has powerful political import—and only a small fragment of its power will ever be realized until that import is broadly understood. Through it democracy itself can be given a new, more human foundation, and form a new, more humanizing lifeworld. As Emerson—in important ways the discoverer and founder of this new form of democracy—put it at the very end of his essay "The American Scholar," in which it was first framed: "The love of [humanity can] be a wall of defense and a wreath of joy around all[:] a nation of [human beings can] for the first time exist, [when] each believes [them]self inspired by the...Soul which also inspires all."

This mediated, aesthetic, and pedagogical reverence, in other words, can be made the ground for *true* human solidarity—true because it involves a *being* true, an *actively* reverent faithfulness, hopefulness, and charitability toward ourselves and one another as we grow involved in aesthetically and pedagogically shared life. We learn to naturally treat others as moral ends-in-themselves as our beings grow together, becoming aesthetically and pedagogically enmeshed: *they* become an inalienable part of *us*. And as we experience/create the harmonic convergence of our personal life paths, the new aesthetic multeity-in-unity of those hitherto separate paths also becomes a new political *e pluribus unum*. A new polity, a new birth of freedom, what Whitman called, "a sublime and serious *Religious* Democracy" in his *Democratic Vistas*—in many ways still the definitive testament of this new polity—is born and brought to light through us.

Since the stakes here are as high as that, we need to carefully ground them, to dig a space where they can be firmly planted. Our ultimate goals here are political and spiritual, but we will only get to the level of actual and authentic democratic spirit by grounding that spirit in the clear understanding, first, of naturally arising psychological and pedagogical phenomena and, then, of ways we can deliberately cultivate these naturally arising phenomena to eventually take political shape and come to spiritual reality. So let's start to do that.

The Security Blanket as the Naturally Arisen Symbol for Interwoven Life

According to the psychoanalyst D. W. Winnicott, children revere their security blankets, their teddy bears, and many other gifts both as symbols of their givers and, at the same time, as vehicles of their own ability to make meaning of the world (Winnicott 1953). These gifts are "transitional objects" through which children experience both their parents' continuing, reassuring presence and their own growing personal freedom.

Transitional objects are pedagogical devices derived from the "alloparenting" (Hrdy 1999) practiced by many primate species, in which nurturance and education are provided by "other parents" than biological mothers and fathers, most often grandmothers. They are objective correlative alloparents. A teddy bear—a gift from a parent or alloparent that becomes a playmate in the parent's absence—allows a child to bring a portion of the world to playful life, infusing it with the life of her imagination. It is at the same time a symbol of a parent, an imaginatively reciprocating friend, and a manifestation of the child's own creative lifeforce. In the imaginative play the child conducts, the customary boundaries between self and world, and self and other, fall away. Through this object, a deep imaginative investment in the world is evoked. The gift of the transitional object becomes a vehicle for the reverent love of its giver toward its receiver to be transformed into the receiver's reverent love for the world, expressed through the prolonged fountain of creative play found through the gift.

This multilayered reverence mediated through the gift is pivotal to the eventual development of democratic, nonauthoritarian reverence. At the outset of the *Emile*, Rousseau makes a key distinction between "the education of men" and "the education of things," and says that the former is to be avoided at all costs in the early education of free, whole human beings. The transitional object is a naturally arising "education of things" that is *also* a nonauthoritarian education offered by persons to other persons, to develop as whole, free beings. It is a natural delivery device for a freeing, imaginative "sentimental education" to very young children. And the transitional space it provides in the breaking down of the boundaries between self, world, and other is the space in which Emerson and Whitman's reverential religious democracy can come to grow, if properly cultivated in educational institutions. The spirit of creative play generated by the transitional object can become the spirit of creative *inter*play of genuine democratic life, if properly nurtured.

Once we see how that spirit is nurtured, first in the teaching of art, then in the art of teaching, we will be able to see something of the kind of educational institutions we will need to nurture a large-scale democracy of mutual reverence, in which this transitional space comes to permeate everyday life.

Implied Creators: Art as Alloparenting for Cultural Attachment and Transitional Experience

All works of art can be considered as transitional objects: as gifts from the past in which we can find present, creative meaning. Since the giver is present *only* in the gift, only indirectly, the receiver of the work of art is free to love it both for its immediate meaning and for the implicit care of the bestower that it manifests.

Our love for "Shakespeare" or "Toni Morrison" or "The Beatles" is stronger for the fact that we love them through the things they have made for and given to us, for us to appropriate meaningfully to ourselves. We love them because their gifts have filled our lives with meaning. John Dewey died the very year Winnicott's essay on the transitional object was published. But an implicit understanding of the deep power and meaning of the transitional object in human life is clearly conveyed in one of the central passages of his *Art as Experience* (1934a): "In the end works of art are the only media of complete and unhindered communication between [human beings] that can occur in a world full of gulfs and walls that limit community of experience."

The experience of art provides us with an elemental way of revering the life we share with others. Because art is a gift of life, an embodied experience given by one person to be experienced, interpreted, and reflected on however a second person sees fit in terms of their own life experience, its meaning is *inherently* shared. When we find meaning in art, we understand implicitly that that meaning has been created by the artist and re-created by us, and so belongs to us both. We don't need to undergo the often difficult deliberative process of coming to agreement before we can be said to share the experience: it is enough to have found some meaning in receiving another's gift. As with the child's appropriation of the security blanket or teddy bear, we infer that the giver's central intent was for us to find our own meaning in their gift. And when we do find meaning in art, a by-product of that meaning is an awe-filled reverence for the communion that has been effected between the artist and ourselves through their gift to us and the meaning we have made of it.

What, then, do we need to *do* to fully cultivate that fully communicative meaning? What attitude toward art maximizes its potential to cultivate reverence for life? Though it is possible to separately idolize the things, the authors, or even our own subjective experience, the fully actualized experience of art can be seen to encompass implicitly each of these three dimensions of reverence. We can even go so far as to say that when we *do* isolate the elements of aesthetic experience, we slip into idolatry of one form or another, and that it is only when we are able to bring these elements fully together that aesthetic experience becomes fully "religious" in Dewey's sense (1934b): offering a creatively mediated "adjustment" between self and world, rather than either an "accommodation" of the self to the world in submissive worship or an "adaptation" of a portion of the world to the self, as "property" admired in a spirit of egoist self-worship.

In this view, the idea of "art for art's sake" is submissively idolatrous; and the idea that "beauty is in the eye of the beholder," that the experience of art is *entirely* subjective, is self-idolatry. In this view, art is fundamentally a nonsectarian religious phenomenon that leads us to live "life for life's sake," in which our individual life-force is engaged in lifeworlds larger than our own current one, and we encounter an expansive sense of life—tacitly recognizing that this sense is in very large part a gift from some author/culture/muse. This magnanimous, expansive sense of life in the transitional space that art provides conveys a reverence for the expansiveness of life itself.

It also conveys a reverence for our own, personal liveliness as integral to the expansiveness of life as a whole. Play with the transitional object offers a magnanimously expansive sense of self: the object is not just an object; it becomes a friend with whom we enter into play, allowing us to see the world in terms of dynamic play in which we take part rather than of static property that is either ours and not others' or others' and not ours. Here we find the psychological origins of what poet/anthropologist Lewis Hyde (1979) has called the "gift economy" that supervenes on the "market economy" of exchanged property. The gift economy is an economy of meaning that is *humanly* productive, in which gifts keep giving, rather than being conceived in terms of mere exchange. This economy of continual giving and receiving is a spiritual economy, not an economy of *mere* "things," mere commodities, but of *living* things, which we invest, both individually and collectively, with life, just as children do their security blankets and teddy bears. And these living things, insofar as we are able to invest them with life, become vehicles of enduring reverential love: love from the absent past that is felt in the immediate present, just as the love of the absent parent is felt in the child's experience of the security blanket and the teddy bear.

Louise Rosenblatt's *The Reader, the Text, and the Poem: The Transactional Theory of the Literary Work* (1978), taking its cue from Dewey's last book, *Knowing and the Known* (Dewey and Bentley 1949), shows how in a literary experience a "poem" is evoked only through a specific reader's singular engagement with a specific text: it is an instance of a person's making of meaning *through* a text, an aesthetic transaction for personal, meaningful transitional experience. Works of art no more have meaning in themselves than teddy bears have life in themselves: they have life only insofar as *we* are able to imaginatively *bring* them to life. Rosenblatt, though, never effectively brought into her understanding of transaction the implicit, yet very powerful connection that readers make with *authors* through texts that Dewey referred to in *Art as Experience*, as important in the experience of art as the tacit realization of the parent's gift is in bringing the teddy bear to life.

In our book *Teaching Literacy for Love and Wisdom: Being the Book and Being the Change* (2011), Jeffrey D. Wilhelm and I use Wayne C. Booth's idea of "the implied author" (1961) to remedy this. In *The Company We Keep* (1988), Booth cites the poet Harold Brodkey: "Reading is an intimate act, perhaps more intimate than any other human act. I say this because of the prolonged (or intense) exposure of one mind to another." And he claims the tacit recognition of the loving presence of authors behind their works makes the experience of art more than either pleasant or useful—more than either *dulce* or *utile*, in the terms Horace famously set forth in *The Art of Poetry*. Art is also lovable, *amabile*, serving to make artists what Aristotle calls "*true* friends"—friends we value for their own sake even more than for the pleasure or use they provide, even if the pleasure and useful insights of art are more immediately palpable than the love we feel for artists.

Most readers—even very young ones—are far more aware of their love for authors through their works than children are consciously aware that they love their parents through their teddy bears, as the many members of the J. K. Rowling and Lemony Snicket fanclubs will readily attest. And this reverential love is perhaps the main force that keeps those of us who still have the habit reading. We keep reading both to keep company with the authors who are among our greatest, most permanent, and wisest and most life-nourishing friends, and to renew our acquaintance with others in "real" life—with those to whom we are more present in chronological time, though less present in imagination—through the wisdom these authors help us find through their sharing of life with us.

To see just *how* we make friends with authors, and through this friendship acquire increased devotion to life, you can undertake a brief poetic experiment by first reading a poem, and then do the following, as, developed in Gabriele Rico's *Creating Re-creations: Inspiration from the Source* (2000): first, make sure you have a timing device with an indicator for seconds on hand, then read the poem slowly to yourself, outloud if you can. Next, read it once again. Circle each word or phrase that particularly resonated with you when you're done reading, or write the words on a separate sheet of paper, with lots of space between them. If you didn't write your words and phrases on a separate sheet of paper earlier, do so now. Circle them. Then write other words or phrases around them, just by free associating with whatever ideas or memories come up for you. This is Gabriele's "clustering" technique that draws on the image-rich right brain with as little interference as possible from the linear left brain. Finally, with your timing device handy, give yourself exactly two-and-a-half minutes to write either a poem or prose poem of your own.

If this exercise worked for you—as Rico's and others' extensive practice reveals it does with astonishing power for most people who undertake it (including, with different poems than this one, very young children)—it made visible the author/reader love that occurs through the poetic generation of meaning through transitional objects. As you reread your chosen poem, you saw, through its words and images, something *in* the author that you admired and thought you could learn from—something the author had to teach you. And when you wrote your poem, you actualized that learning, taking the meaning you found and making it *yours*—or, rather, both yours and the author's.

Further, if you compare your poem to other "re-creations" of that same poem, you'll see how your own meaning-making processes come into play with others', and how the relatedness of those processes evokes reverence for the life you've shared by seeing how your lives have been brought into play through the shared transitional space of the poem. Eight examples—including a poem I myself wrote are offered in Wilhelm and Novak (2011). (It can also be found in the materials for the 2011 conference that launched the book at www.aepl.org.) You may well also wish to try the exercise with your own students and have them compare what they wrote, and what they thought of the author's poem as they wrote.

Here is where we make the bridge from art to teaching. The process through which you took the author's creation in and made new meaning out of it was one in which a certain kind of teacher/student relationship is forged, as is described by Robert Inchausti in his *Spitwad Sutras: Classroom Teaching as Sublime Vocation* (1993): "a *real* teacher takes one's very *life* up into speech, so that others can do the same." In this kind of teaching, whether it occurs through art or through teaching itself, a reverence for both the author/teacher's life and the reader/student's life is evoked. For *new* life has been evoked by their temporary sharing of life, as you yourself experienced in the writing of your poem, if this exercise worked for you. And it is the miraculousness of this new life that is particularly deserving of reverence: the fact that new life has been created from a set of black spots on a white page, and that through this transubstantiation, life itself has vibrantly kept on going, has blossomed anew.

Repeated experiences of the meaningful, poetic generation of new life thus bring about not just *personal* attachment between authors and readers, and teachers and students, but more general forms of *cultural* attachment: the understanding of the meaning of our own and others' life as the conversion of inheritances we reap from the past into legacies we bestow to the future. Think of your favorite author or your favorite teacher, what they have meant to your life, and how you have lived that life to embody that meaning for others, to make of it what *they* will—and you'll immediately see what this means. As both a personal and a pertinent example, I have come to see my love for Shakespeare (helped along by many teachers, actors, directors, theatrical institutions, and literary critics) centering on the idea of "the marriage of true minds" from Sonnet 116—despite *all* the many kinds of "impediments" that exist to the consummation of such marriages, as are powerfully exemplified dramatically in his plays—as a central historic seed of this very theory, which I am now giving to you to make what you will of.

As Dewey remarked in *Art as Experience*, this "marriage of true minds" occurs most naturally and perhaps most fully, through the creation and experience of art, where it is mediated through the created thing, the transitional object. But the transitional object is not the only source of what Winnicott called "transitional space," the space where self, world, and others are brought to flow together. Transitional space between and among persons is created whenever any of us, under any circumstances, "takes our life up into speech, so that others may do the same." It is the space of wise, artful teaching, wherever it occurs, the space where we come alive for one another. In art, we come to be present for one another, but at a spatial and temporal distance. In teaching, we seek to become *directly* present for others, to make our *immediate* experience together come into artful flow. Teaching is where we bring the lessons of art to life, where transitional space is created, not just in the imagination, but in reality. And it is where the complex, mediated reverence of art becomes immediate without losing its personal and temporal complexity. The experience of the gift of teaching, like that of the gift of art, comes from one person's "taking their life up into speech" acquiring some meaningful bearing on another's future. And that personal, reverential bearing is what differentiates personal teaching from impersonal instruction.

Implied Teachers: Moving beyond Competitive "Cur-riculum" toward Amative "Ami-culum"

The best teachers know that they profoundly love their students. They know that at least some, if not all of their students, profoundly love them. And they know—beyond this and more importantly—that *through* this very special and powerful love that their students have been helped to love one another, other people the students encounter, and life itself.

Teaching is both an important form of love and an important vehicle for it. And if this reverential love could somehow learn how to publicly and proudly speak its name—in some ways, the central aim of this book—we might be able to find a way to publicly make education something much, much more than the loveless, mechanical impartation of impersonal knowledge and skills it has now mostly become. We might be able to imbue both education—and through education, democratic life—with meaning, making them forms of meaningful communication, not of at best submissive, idolatrously worshipful inculcation, and at worst meaningless, manipulative drivel. If what Inchausti calls *real* teaching can become the expected norm rather than the dramatic exception, we might be able to turn the cultural attachment that art provides into reverential cherishment for education and for democratic life. No small feat.

But what would it take, realistically, to do that? Right now, we basically have two opposite models of teaching, neither of which in itself accounts for the aesthetic phenomenon of *inter*personal communication. One is more traditionally "masculine" in nature: the sublime "sage on the stage" directly conveying powerful thoughts. The other is more traditionally "feminine" in nature: the empathically selfless listener to "the sound on the ground" of students' voices. Nothing is inherently wrong with either of these models, but perhaps the best of both can be combined through a third one, which—drawing on the understanding of aesthetic transitional space we developed in the last section—we might (with the help of Hansen, 2001) call "the art of the heart": teaching understood as meaningful interpersonal communication mediated, not through *things* per se, but through *experiences* made by one person for others to make their own meaning out of.

Teachers, besides interacting directly with students in various ways, are the implied authors of the activities they construct for students to learn through. Insofar as the learning that transpires through those activities is not just useful but personally meaningful, they are artists of the mind and heart, helping people different from themselves bring the world to life for themselves and one another, through these experiences embodying what they find personally meaningful. Teachers whose practice is centered in this mode evoke the same complex reverence artists do. All wrapped up together is reverence for the thing learned, reverence for the renewal of personal experience that learning evokes, and also—implicitly but all the more powerfully for its indirectness and experiential complexity—reverence for the person who devised the learning experience.

In the personally transformative teaching experience described at the outset of this essay, the serious fun I saw my students having in the activity I'd designed for them—the creative personal interplay of the historically given subject matter, the activity I'd artistically constructed around it, and the meaning they made together through creatively participating in this live experience—reverence was being paid to the subject matter, to their own creativity, and also to me, the person who elicited this creativity by devising the experience that brought the subject matter to life. Paul Woodruff (2001) speaks of "home" as the central place where reverence is paid. This activity helped the students feel at home with each other, with the world of the subject matter, and with me, the person who had helped them feel that the portion of the world we were studying was an important part of their home—an inheritance given personally *to them* through the activity, in which they could live together, and through which, perhaps, their future lives would also grow more meaningful. The activity took something from the past and helped the students feel at home in it; and this, perhaps, helped them learn, as they continued on with their lives, to feel more at home with the world in general.

Both because teachers teach directly as well as indirectly—as opposed to artists, whose work is most often confined to communicable media detached from themselves—and because they often, also as opposed to most artists, tend to have self-effacing personalities, the artful component of teaching is often deemphasized in favor either of effective instruction in a given subject matter or of effective care for individual students. But in the end this artfulness might be the most effective means for the achievement of both of these other ends—as well as effecting an end in itself of newly shared life, by bringing people's lives directly into play with one another.

Let me speak personally here again, about one of my own teachers, in the hope that the things I say will evoke memories of some of your own most important teachers and teaching experiences. The single most influential teacher for me in this regard was Jerrold McGann, whose two-term freshman Humanities course centering on the question "What is wisdom literature?" galvanized my thinking in a way no other course before or since has—and is as much the personal origin of the ideas I'm sharing with you in this essay as Shakespeare's idea of "the marriage of true minds" is its historical origin. Decades down the road now, I can still vividly remember just about every book I read and every paper I wrote for that class, and how I was changed by them. I've experienced better-conducted interpersonal discussions and felt more personally attended to in other classes, but if there was a single class that made me the person I am today, it was that one. And it did so through a carefully scaffolded structure of readings and writing assignments that experientially conveyed the power of texts—among them Thoreau's *Walden*, selections from Montaigne's *Essays* (most prominently the final one, "Of Experience"), Austen's *Pride and Prejudice*, Melville's *Moby-Dick*, and Wittgenstein's *Philosophical Investigations*—that were a hybrid of thinking and feeling, and as such conveyed what it meant to lead a life of both personal and more than personal wisdom. In retrospect, it was no accident—though the fact of it dawned on me only quite recently—that my following a personal calling to teach led me eventually to fashion a course for teachers that brought them both to encounter some of the best wisdom literature about teaching and to write and live wisdom literature of their own (See Novak 2009, 2010; Wilhelm and Novak 2011).

I've been lucky enough to have been taught to teach creatively, to have taught mostly in places that have given me a large amount of freedom to teach as I saw fit, and also to have had the freedom to leave when that freedom was constricted for one reason or another. Imagine, though, what teaching could become if all teachers were trained in large part as artists are. If the *norm* for teacher education was the conservatory, where knowledge, skills, and traditions are rigorously taught, but in the service of cultivating individual character and talent (Botstein 1997; Novak 2010). And if the norm for teaching in schools was not "instructional" (though certainly instructional standards can't be discarded, only subordinated to higher, *human* standards, as techniques like intonation and drawing are in the teaching of art) but one of the cultivation of aesthetic reverence for life through the artful devising of aesthetic experiences allowing us to take up life together with one another. Something tells me that if this were the case, we wouldn't have nearly the problem we do retaining teachers in the profession or convincing people to pay them adequately for what they do. We would have a profession made up of what Inchausti called "real teachers" who "take up their very lives into speech so others may do the same." And the profession of teaching would for the first time be a real profession.

Creative teachers and creative teaching would also *matter*, more than just about anything, not just in the ability of students to negotiate life creatively and humanly, but in our collective ability to come to matter for one another as human beings and to live together collectively in a human and creative manner. As we move from models of education focused on standardized "curriculum," literally, in its etymology, a "race course" and toward what we might newly label reverential "amiculum," the course of bringing to life loving friendship—both directly among individuals who are present to one another and implicitly toward those living in the past and the future—we will create at the same time the new democracy described—with help from Emerson, Whitman, and Dewey—at the outset of this essay. As we move from an education policy of "No Child Left Behind in the Race to Nowhere"—the policy of the manipulative mobilization of populaces of all empires past and present—toward an education policy of "Each Person Drawn Forward to a Life of Creative Responsiveness and Responsibility"—the policy of all cultures of wisdom, though never *yet* effectively instituted within broad democratic political life (see Novak and Wilhelm 2011, Chapter 9, "Aesthetic Humanity: The History, and Possible Future, of Wisdom")—we at the same time collectively create *creative* democracy, which empowers individuals to unite effectively and lovingly with one another. We create democracy writ large, in which mutual self-government on a large scale can for the first time genuinely occur, because citizens are deliberately engaged from their earliest years, and throughout their education, in the psychological, aesthetic, and pedagogical processes through which self-government writ small naturally occurs (see Martin 2008): a democracy in which the virtue of reverentially recognizing and learning from the gifts of others has become a fundamental habit of everyday life.

Everyone a Teacher:
How the Recognition of Implied Authorship and Teacherhood Can Make Us All the Implied Citizens of Whitman's "Sublime and Serious, Religious Democracy"

Jane Addams once said that it was only when the cultural forces of democracy grew stronger than its commercial forces that we would have *actual* democracy (Seigfried 2006). In our terms, only when a transactional gift economy is made to prevail over the interactive market economy, when democratic friendship for its own sake prevails over mere relations of employment and pleasure, of production and consumption, will we have collectively created an *e pluribus unum* that reflects the ideal of unity that Paul Woodruff claims to be the ultimate object of the virtue of reverence. The temporary condition of aesthetic "multeity in unity" can eventually become a relatively stable condition of political *"e pluribus unum"*: a condition in which we feel mutually recognized as human beings as we go about the ordinary processes of life, in which the large, public world—as well as certain special spaces in our small, private worlds—feels like "home," the place where Woodruff says, "we know reverence at first hand."

Reverence is not just an ethic. We have seen how it also lays out for us a poetics and a politics, when we see life as a gift, to be reverently received and given reverently again. As we learn to make meaning through others' gifts—first through those given personally and intentionally to us, as transitional objects and transitional space, by those who play a mentoring role in our lives; then through those we evoke directly by reaching out to others in our daily existence—a world of poetic meaning forms and grows. That world has no firm boundaries; it is capable of infinite expansion. The gift economy is richer and more powerful than the market economy: its riches are real, human riches, not artificial value; its power is real, human power, not imaginary status. As we learn to more thoroughly embody this gift economy in our educational institutions, both in and out of schools, its meaning may eventually even loosen the grip of the seemingly all-consuming market economy that has now reached into our schools and the lives of students and teachers everywhere, and which has no reverence for either human or natural life. But that day will come only as, one by one, we seek to "take our very lives up into speech, so that others may do the same": to live life as much as possible as a reverential politics of meaningful gifts, in which everyone and every thing is our teacher.

References

Booth, W. C. 1961. *The Rhetoric of Fiction.* Chicago: University of Chicago Press.

———. 1988. *The Company We Keep: An Ethics of Fiction.* Berkeley: University of California Press.

Botstein, L. 1997. "The Development of Talent and the Reforming of Secondary Education: A University President's Perspective." Paper delivered at the

annual meeting of the American Educational Research Association, Chicago, March.
Dewey, J. 1934a. *Art as Experience.* New York: Minton, Balch.
———. 1934b. *A Common Faith.* New Haven: Yale University Press.
Dewey, J., and A. Bentley. 1949. *Knowing and the Known.* Boston: Beacon Press.
Hansen, D. T. 2001. *Exploring the Moral HeART of Teaching: Toward a Teacher's Creed.* New York: Teachers College Press.
Hrdy, S. B. 1999. *Mother Nature: A History of Mothers, Infants, and Natural Selection.* New York: Pantheon.
Hyde, L. 1983. *The Gift: Imagination and the Erotic Life of Property.* New York: Random House.
Inchausti, R. L. 1993. *Spitwad Sutras: Classroom Teaching as Sublime Vocation.* Westport, CT: Bergin & Garvey.
Martin, J. R. 2008. "Education Writ Large." In *Education and the Making of a Democratic People.* Edited by J. I. Goodlad, R. Soder, and B. McDaniel, 47–64. Boulder, CO: Paradigm.
Novak, B. 2009. "The Audacity of thought: Seeing thinking as the moral virtue required for the Refounding of Democracy on a Moral Basis. *Studies in Philosophy and Education,* 40: 83–93.
———. 2010. "Up from Normal School: A Transactional, Aesthetic, Wisdom-Centered Foundation of Education for Teachers to Educate a Nation of Free, Humane Persons Less at Risk of Self-enslavement." Presentation at the Critical Issues in Education Conference, Chicago, November.
Rico, G. L. 2000. *Creating Re-creations: Inspiration from the Source.* Second Edition. Spring, TX: Absey.
Rosenblatt, L. M. 1978. *The Reader, the Text, and the Poem: The Transactional Theory of the Literary Work.* Carbondale: Southern Illinois University Press.
Seigfried, C. H. 2006. "The John Dewey Address." Paper presented at the annual meeting of the American Educational Research Association, San Francisco, March.
Wilhelm, J. D., and B. Novak. 2011. *Teaching Literacy for Love and Wisdom: Being the Book and Being the Change.* New York: Teachers College Press.
Winnicott, D. W. 1953. Transitional objects and transitional phenomena: A study of the first not-me possession. *International Journal of Psycho-Analysis* 34: 89–97.
Woodruff, P. 2001. *Reverence: Renewing a Forgotten Virtue.* New York: Oxford University Press.

Index

art 15, 135–6, 153–4, 156–8, 160–1, 163
awe
   in Kant (Achtung) 138, 143–4
   reverent 4–5

beliefs 4, 11, 41, 70, 137
Brooks, Gwendolyn 134–5

cardinal virtue 5–6
Carini, Patricia 79–81
ceremony 3, 35, 114, 149–50
classroom
   community 1, 8, 14, 108
   reverent 7–8, 12, 14
   teaching 1, 63
Codell, Esme R. 2–4, 16
commitment to teaching 68, 74, 94, 153
compassion 2, 6–7, 27, 94
connection 6, 14, 79, 84, 100, 121
Cuban, Larry 67
culture of school 51, 99

democracy 16, 130, 139, 154, 164
Dewey, John 22, 28, 66, 69, 79, 81, 83, 156–8
Dillard, Annie 54–5, 75, 94
duty 5–6, 97, 111, 138, 144

Edmundson, Mark 42–6
Emerson, Ralph Waldo 10, 17, 25, 99, 104, 154
emotions 2–3, 5–8, 21, 34, 37, 65
epiphany 12–13, 63–6, 71–5

ethics 5–6, 165
experience
   aesthetic 142, 157, 163
   lived 82, 95, 104, 119–20, 123

gift economy versus market economy 157–8, 165
gifts 10, 12, 155–6, 165

Hansen, David T. 13, 66, 81, 84, 90, 162

irreverence 9

Jackson, Philip W. 68, 73
justice 3–5, 126, 131, 143

Kant, Immanuel 15, 138–9, 142–5
Kozol, Jonathan 125

listening 10, 18–22, 41, 44, 53–5, 70, 89
love
   as agape 5
   attentive 11, 34, 36–40, 42, 46
   as eros 5, 27
   unconditional 5, 11

Murdoch, Iris 15, 36, 40–2, 138, 142

Neiman, Susan 50, 54–5, 60

pedagogy 71, 134, 139
progressive education 33, 122
Prospect School 79–80, 82–8, 91–4

Random Harvest (film) 17, 27, 31
reverence
  in community 3–7, 9, 72, 100, 111
  definition of 2–3
  and human limitations 3, 10–11, 34, 42, 80, 82, 150
  and humility 10, 25
  and laughter 10, 25–6
  objects of 14, 113, 125
  and respect 5–7, 42, 50, 129, 139, 143
reverent
  experience 4, 82
  listening 20–1
  teaching 10–11, 17–18, 21, 23, 26–8, 59
reverential
  love 159, 161
  silence 53, 55, 59
Ruddick, Sara 36–7, 39

Schweitzer, Albert 7
shame 2–3, 5–7, 9–11, 34, 80
silence 1, 10–12, 49–51, 55–60, 98–9

sublime 15, 75, 138–9, 142–6, 150
suffering 7, 53, 59, 144

teacher education 50, 163
teachers
  elementary school 117–18, 120–2, 124
  loving 45
  most important 163
  passionate 11
  reverential 38
  silent 59
  virtuous 6

vocation 63, 66, 69, 71, 75

Weil, Simone 15, 36–9, 53–4, 146, 150
Whitman, Walt 15, 98–9, 107, 112, 124, 155–6, 164
Woodruff, Paul 3, 34–6, 49, 59, 138, 149–50, 162
Wordsworth, William 62, 64, 68–9

GPSR Compliance

The European Union's (EU) General Product Safety Regulation (GPSR) is a set of rules that requires consumer products to be safe and our obligations to ensure this.

If you have any concerns about our products, you can contact us on

ProductSafety@springernature.com

In case Publisher is established outside the EU, the EU authorized representative is:

Springer Nature Customer Service Center GmbH
Europaplatz 3
69115 Heidelberg, Germany

www.ingramcontent.com/pod-product-compliance
Lightning Source LLC
LaVergne TN
LVHW051911060526
838200LV00004B/92